MY FAVORITE ILLUSTRATIONS

My FAVORITE ILLUSTRATIONS

HERSCHEL H. HOBBS

RONALD K. BROWN, COMPILER

BROADMAN PRESS
NASHVILLE, TENNESSEE

0-8054-2209-9
Dewey Decimal Classification: 251.08
Subject Heading:
ILLUSTRATIONS // SERMONS
Library of Congress
Catalog Card Number: 89-37250

Printed in the United States of America

The material in this book is reprinted and adapted from *Studying Life and Work Lessons* ©
Copyright by Convention Press and The Sunday School Board of the Southern Baptist
Convention.

Unless otherwise noted, all Scripture quotations are from the *Revised Standard Version of
the Bible,* copyrighted 1946, 1952, © 1971, 1973. Used by permission.

Scripture quotations marked (KJV) are from the *King James Version.*

Library of Congress Cataloging-in-Publication Data
Hobbs, Herschel H.
   My favorite illustrations / Herschel H. Hobbs ; Ronald K. Brown,
compiler.
     p. cm.
  ISBN 0-8054-2209-9
  1. Homiletical illustrations. I. Brown, Ronald K., 1946–
BV4225.2.H63 1990
  251'.08—dc20   89-37250
                                            CIP

With love and thanksgiving this volume is dedicated to Connie, who illustrates for me the beautiful qualities of womanhood described in Proverbs 31:10-31

RONALD K. BROWN

Preface

We are a visual people who know well the meaning of the old adage, "A picture is worth a thousand words." We spend countless hours viewing television, watching videos, looking at photographs, sightseeing, and engaging in other visual activities. As a result, we have replaced the art of conversation with the visual, for we have discovered we generally enjoy looking more than listening.

While I, too, enjoy the visual, as a person who has worked with words most all his adult life, I also appreciate a well-turned phrase, a poignant comment, and a penetrating word. A well-constructed, colorful, and insightful picture in words can be deeply moving and stimulating.

This book is about word pictures. Usually we refer to them as illustrations—those stories, anecdotes, and concise statements that bring vitality to speeches, sermons, lessons, and other verbal presentations. Most persons who speak or write are constantly on the look for illustrations. They know the value of an appropriate illustration and season their works with them.

Although we may not like to admit it, our listeners or readers tend to remember our stories more than they do the points of our outlines. The theme of many a sermon or lesson has been forgotten while a meaningful illustration has been indelibly printed in one's memory.

Dr. Herschel H. Hobbs understands the value of potent illustrations. He has been a respected and effective preacher for over sixty years. He is also a prolific writer with over 125 books to his credit. Whether speaking or writing, Dr. Hobbs includes illustrative material to support the theme of his messages and to enlighten his audience.

This book has been developed from Dr. Hobbs's contribution as a writer. For over twenty-two years he has authored *Studying*

Adult Life and Work Lessons, a Bible study commentary based on the Life and Work Curriculum Series produced by The Sunday School Board of the Southern Baptist Convention. The commentary has been extremely popular since its inception and sells nearly 100,000 copies each quarter. The popularity of the commentary is a tribute to Dr. Hobbs's appealing style of writing and his outstanding skills in biblical exposition. He has the ability to take profound truth of Scripture and translate it into terms with which we all can identify and resonate.

My Favorite Illustrations is a compilation of illustrations Dr. Hobbs has used in *Studying Adult Life and Work Lessons*. Included are anecdotes, quotations, and poems.

Dr. Hobbs once told me he did not maintain an illustration file as such. He gleans support material from reading, stories he has heard, and personal experiences. Examples of the different types and sources will be readily identified as you peruse this volume.

Over the years one source book has been a favorite of Dr. Hobbs. *I Quote*, edited by Virginia Ely (Fleming H. Revell Co.: Old Tappan, New Jersey, 1947) is a collection of poems and quotations on miscellaneous topics. Dr. Hobbs also employs other anthologies and collections of wit and wisdom.

A valuable by-product of **My Favorite Illustrations** is the autobiographical nature of many of the stories. Although he would not acknowledge the word, Herschel Hobbs is a *giant* in his denomination. He has both witnessed and made denominational history.

He speaks from personal experience about such outstanding personalities as Greek New Testament scholar Dr. A. T. Robertson; the illustrious pastors of First Baptist Church, Dallas, Texas, Dr. George W. Truett and long-time friend Dr. W. A. Criswell; and many other persons of renown in Christian circles.

In several of the illustrations Dr. Hobbs relates his recollection of major occurrences in the life of his denomination, including his eighteen years as preacher on "The Baptist Hour" and his tenure as president of the Southern Baptist Convention.

You also will note that Dr. Hobbs has the insight to use common situations to teach a spiritual truth. As he does, he models for us how to use our own personal experiences as illustrations for preaching and teaching.

Honesty and openness characterize some of the incidents. The emotion is evident as he refers to his dear wife, Frances, who went to be with the Lord in 1984. Obviously she was a beloved helpmate in his ministry.

As I suggested above, not all the items included in this volume are original with Dr. Hobbs. He often cites literary greats, other preachers, and teachers. Some of the anecdotes and jokes have been around for years, but they still have value and may not be familiar to younger preachers and teachers.

Many items are about preachers. Since Dr. Hobbs is a preacher and thrilled with it, you could expect no less. I also have included several statements that declare the eternal truths of the gospel in Dr. Hobbs's own unique way. He has that ability to paint marvelous word pictures.

The illustrations are classified by general topics. However, many of them may relate to several topics. Furthermore, you will see how certain entries may be used in ways that differ from what I have suggested or from how Dr. Hobbs originally used them. He has repeated some of the items over the years, but in applying them to different situations, they assume freshness and new meaning. In some cases a Scripture reference is included, and a simple application has been provided.

As in any endeavor of worth, no one can claim full credit for an achievement. I know with certainty that I am indebted to several persons who encouraged and assisted me in this project. A thank-you does not seem sufficient, but I trust those persons will sense the depth of my feelings.

Of course, I acknowledge the valuable contribution of Herschel Hobbs and the encouragement he gave when I first approached him about the project. To edit his work in *Studying Adult Life and Work Lessons* for these past two years has been a personal privilege and delight.

I thank Michael Fink, manager, Adult Life and Work Curriculum Section, Baptist Sunday School Board, for his valued support. Actually, the idea for this compilation came from a conversation with him. I also appreciate other management personnel at the Board who gave their approval for my use of the previously published material. A caring work-family like the Baptist Sunday School Board is rare indeed.

I also thank the editorial staff of Broadman Press for their enthusiastic reception of the book idea and then for their patience with its novice compiler.

My wife Connie has been invaluable to me, as always. She input material, printed and proofed drafts, and most importantly, she challenged and encouraged me when deadlines were hanging mercilessly over my head.

Whether you use these illustrations for preaching or teaching or merely for the reading, my hope is that they will be pictures in words that guide you in your understanding and application of the Word.

To God be the glory!

RONALD K. BROWN

Contents

ACHIEVEMENT/SUCCESS

Ah, but a man's reach should exceed his grasp,
Or what's a heaven for?
—Robert Browning

Someone said, "Poor eyes limit your sight; poor vision limits your deeds."

A vision without a task is a dream;
A task without a vision is drudgery;
A vision and a task is the hope of the world.
—Anonymous

'Tis looking downward makes one dizzy.
—Robert Browning

I will study and get ready and the opportunity will come.
—Abraham Lincoln

The secret of success in life is for a man to be ready for his opportunity when it comes.
—Benjamin Disraeli

We live in deeds, not years; in thought, not breath;
In feelings, not in figures on a dial.
We should count time by heart-throbs. He most lives
Who thinks most, feels the noblest, acts the best.
Life's but a means unto an end; that end
Beginning, mean, and end of all things—God.
—Phillip James Bailey

That man may last, but never lives,
Who much receives, but nothing gives;
Whom none can love, whom none can thank,

Creation's blot, creation's blank.

—Thomas Gibbons, "When Jesus Dwelt"

If you can sit at set of sun
And count the deeds that you have done
And counting find
One self-denying act, one word
That eased the heart of him that heard,
One glance most kind,
Which fell like sunshine where he went,
Then you may count that day well spent.

—Robert Browning

Essentials for Greatness

Many years ago I wrote a book called *Moses' Mighty Men*. The thesis of the book was that at the human level three things are essential to make a person great. A person must be endowed with the capacity for greatness; the person must live in a historical environment that calls forth greatness; the person must be surrounded by lesser greats who contribute to another's greatness.

However, we cannot ignore the place God fills in producing a great person. For without His power and grace all human efforts will prove futile.

Opportunities, Hopes, and Dreams

On the last day of the year a celebration is held throughout the land. Beginning at the stroke of midnight in Times Square in New York City, the multitudes cheer, horns sound, whistles blow, and people laugh and cry for joy. Amidst the celebration are the shouts of "Happy New Year!" This spectacle is repeated in succession in the various time zones from the Atlantic Seaboard to the far western reaches of Hawaii. We say, "A New Year has come!" For us a new year symbolizes new opportunities, new hopes, and new dreams.

And yet, the stroke of the hour simply has marked the dawning of another day. Whether the year really will be *new* lies within each person. If, when the shouting is over, we fall back into the same old rut of sin and rebellion against God, then nothing has changed. No, years become new only if we make them so. Resolutions for new days, new beginnings, opportunities, and dreams are not to be made only in the excitement of the moment; but long after the glamor is gone these resolutions are to become the order of each day.

This Is Success

He has achieved success who has lived well, laughed often and loved much; who has gained the respect of intelligent men, and the love of little children; who has filled his niche and accomplished his task; who has left the world better than he found it, whether by an improved poppy, a perfect poem, or a rescued soul; who has never lacked appreciation of earth's beauty, or failed to express it; who has always looked for the best in others, and given the best he had; whose life was an inspiration; whose memory a benediction.
—Thomas Stanley

Always a Success

Thomas A. Edison was the most prolific inventor in modern times—perhaps ever. He made scores of attempts to invent the light bulb. After an unsuccessful effort, one of his associates said, "Well, you have failed again." "No," replied Edison, "I have succeeded again. I now know another way how not to invent a light bulb."

God's Hand Is on Him

Many times I have been asked how I explain Billy Graham's successful work. I could mention his ability as a preacher, his co-laborers, and the effectiveness of prayerful organization. But my reply is, "God has His hand on him." That's the difference between success and failure in the Lord's work.

ATTITUDE

Someone said that a kicking mule cannot pull, but a pulling mule does not kick.

A. T. Robertson used to tell his students that the Pharisees could split a hair six ways and still have some hair left. I am convinced some Pharisees still exist.

Victims of Their Own Doing

Some people approach life with an attitude that makes for hard going. They were born in the "objective case" and the "kickative mode." They always have a chip on their shoulders and dare anyone to knock it off.

Such people may claim, "God made me this way." Well, I do not agree. Actually, they are victims of their own doing. They never grew out of the "brat" stage of childhood. They are unhappy and make everyone else about them unhappy. These people are sand in the gears of life.

What a World It Would Be

One mind-set says people are to fight for their own rights. People with this mind-set keep books on everything bad ever done to them. Instead of living by Christian love, they live by an *eye for an eye, a tooth for a tooth* morality. Such people are their own worst enemies. They make life miserable for themselves and for everyone else. If everyone lived this way, we would live in a jungle of tooth and talon.

A Jealous Attitude

Like unseen termites, jealousy eats away the very foundation of the social order until the entire structure falls.

Could It Be Me?

If something is wrong with your church and you wonder why, the place to start seeking an answer is with yourself. Is your church unfriendly? What about you? Is it unconcerned about the lost? Are you? Is it behind on its budget requirements? Are you behind, or are you penny-pinching in your giving? Is there hostility in the fellowship? What of your attitude and behavior? You may or may not find the answers within yourself. Nevertheless, you need to be certain you are not part of the problem before you begin pointing an accusing finger at others.

"Ride the Wild Horses"

I recall reading a sermon that likened our emotions to wild horses. Instead of letting our emotions run wild, destroying us and others, we are to *ride* or control our emotions so that they serve us and bless others. "Speaking one's mind" is not a virtue if in doing such we inflict injury.

BIBLE/GOD'S WORD

The New Testament is the *flower* of which the Old Testament is the *bud*.

Fires of iniquity may burn Bibles, evil hearts may deny its truth; but they do not destroy it or evade its message. The Word of God endures forever!

After reading the doctrine of Plato, Socrates, or Aristotle, we feel that the specific difference between their words and Christ's is the difference between inquiry and revelation.
—Joseph Parker

When you have read the Bible you will know it is the Word of God because you will have found it the key to your own heart, your own happiness and your own duty.
—Woodrow Wilson

Willard Johnson on the Bible

Generations follow generations—yet it lives.
Nations rise and fall—yet it lives.
Kings, dictators, presidents come and go—yet it lives.
Torn, condemned, burned—yet it lives.
Doubted, suspected, criticized—yet it lives.
Damned by atheists—yet it lives.
Exaggerated by fanatics—yet it lives.
Misconstrued and misstated—yet it lives.
Its inspiration denied—yet it lives.
Yet it lives—a lamp to our feet,
              a light to our paths,
              a standard for childhood,
              a guide for youth,

a comfort for the aged,
food for the hungry,
water for the thirsty,
rest for the weary,
light for the heathen,
salvation for the sinner,
grace for the Christian.
To know it is to love it;
To love it is to accept it;
To accept it means life eternal.

God's Word in History

The Bible was wrought out in the arena of history. If it is impossible to fathom its message apart from ancient history, it is also true that a person cannot plumb the depths of the meaning of ancient history apart from the Bible. For that matter, to understand history subsequent to the first century, even today, it must be seen in the light of God's Word.

The Bible and Science

Although the Bible contains no proven scientific error, it is not a science textbook. The Bible is a book of religion. Science is concerned with *what*; the Bible is concerned with *Who*.

Endurability of God's Laws

Persons do not *break* the Ten Commandments any more than they break the law of gravity. However, persons are broken by them if they live contrary to their intended purpose.

The Value of the Word

Daniel Webster said, "If we abide by the principles taught in the Bible, our country will go on prospering and to prosper, but if we and our posterity neglect its instruction and authority, no man can tell how sudden a catastrophe may overwhelm us and bury our glory in profound obscurity."

Stay on Base

Theology is somewhat like the game of baseball. In baseball a runner must keep one foot on base or else risk being thrown out. In theology the *base* is the Bible.

The Need for the Word

If truth be not diffused, error will be; if God and His Word are not known and received, the devil and his works will gain the ascendancy; if the evangelical volume does not reach every hamlet, the pages of the corrupt and licentious literature will; if the power of the gospel is not felt through the length and breadth of the land, anarchy and misrule, degradation and misery, corruption and darkness, will reign without mitigation or end.

—Daniel Webster

It Will Come to Pass

One characteristic of prophecy is that its fulfillment is not limited to the time period in which it is uttered. Prophecy telescopes time as humanity sees it to declare the purposes of God that are not limited by the calendar. So while we may see roots of the prophecy in a given time span, the full realization lies in a future uncharted by humankind.

Reading prophecy is like looking at a distant mountain peak while soaring aloft in an airplane. We discover that many mountain ranges are between us and the distant peak we are focusing on. Thus we are to view prophecy from God's vantage point, not ours.

God Said It

Through the years I have tried to be an expository preacher. Occasionally someone will come to take exception to something in the sermon. Believing that I have faithfully drawn the truth from the Word, I say, "Well, I suggest you take that up with the Lord. I didn't say it of myself. I simply told you what God said in His Book."

Bible as Progressive Revelation

We speak of God's *progressive revelation*. This does not mean God began to reveal Himself crudely and learned to do a better job as He went along. Genesis is as much His revelation as is John. Progressive revelation means God revealed Himself progressively to people as they were able to grasp and understand Him. Thus we have a clearer revelation of God in John than in Genesis, but the same God is revealed in both books.

How would Einstein teach arithmetic to a small child? He would not start out with the equation for the theory of relativity or for splitting the atom. He would begin with two plus two equals four. That is not all the arithmetic he knows; but that is as much as the child can grasp. Years later he would teach the child, now an adult, about complex theories. This is also how God revealed Himself to humanity. He did not reveal everything about Himself at one time. He did it gradually.

BROTHERHOOD

Is thy heart right, as my heart is with thine?
Dost thou love and serve God? It is enough
I give thee the right hand of fellowship.
—John Wesley

Prejudice is man-made, not God-made, but only God can help us overcome it.

Equal rights is a blade that cuts both ways. It protects the innocent and punishes the guilty.

The Same Commander

During World War II the Allied Forces were composed of the armies of many nations. None of the armies renounced its own identity, but together they defeated Hitler and his allies. How? They had one greater loyalty and goal. So must the army of the redeemed follow their commander, Jesus Christ, with full assurance of victory over the evil one.

Prejudice Removed in Christ

According to Ephesians 2:14, Christ has removed the "middle wall" that separated Jews and Gentiles. Paul was alluding to the Temple in Jerusalem. The Temple was divided into various courts or sections: Gentiles, Women, Israel, Priests, Holy Place, and Holy of Holies. Gentiles were not allowed beyond the first court.

On the wall beside each entrance into the court of women were stone slabs warning Gentiles not to go beyond that point. One such slab was discovered in 1871 and is in the Museum of the Ancient Oriental in Istanbul. Part of another is in the British Museum. The whole slab reads, "No foreigner may enter within the balustrade and enclosure around the Sanctuary. Whoever is caught will render himself liable to the death penalty which will inevitably follow" (Jack Finegan, *Light from the Ancient Past* [Princeton: Princeton University Press, 1959], 325). Paul used this well-known fact to illustrate the truth that in Christ such estrangement and prejudice are removed.

Prejudice Is Widespread

Flying from Benares to New Delhi, India, Frances and I were given a newspaper printed in English. Not having seen one in several weeks, we devoured almost every word in it.

One section particularly intrigued us. Parents, through small ads, announced they had either a *beautiful* daughter or *handsome* son eligible for marriage. We laughed over the apparent fact that India had no ugly young people.

Most of all we were interested in the words at the end of each ad: "Caste no object," or else the name of a particular caste was given. The inclusion of a caste name meant that people of any other caste need not apply. Here was an example of prejudice among people.

Basis for Racial Harmony

Here are three simple rules that form the basis for racial harmony.
1. All persons have a common origin: God.
2. All persons have a common need: God.
3. All persons have a common purpose: God

Polish but Don't Pray

Can you believe this happened? A white pastor entered the place of worship one weekday to find the black janitor on his knees at the altar. When he was asked what he was doing, the man replied, "I am polishing the brass on the altar rail." "Well, all right," the pastor replied, "but don't let me catch you praying there!"

An Experience of Brotherhood

In 1965 Dr. William R. Tolbert, Jr., an African, was elected president of the Baptist World Alliance. I was a asked to serve as vice-president. Although I was hesitant to accept since I had many other commitments, I feared that my refusal to serve would be misunderstood. Some would have thought that a white Southern Baptist just did not want to serve under a black African. So, I accepted the position.

Those five years were filled with great blessing. Chief among them was the relationship that grew between the Tolberts and the Hobbses. From mere acquaintances we became warm friends. When Frances and I looked at Bill and Victoria Tolbert, we did not see two black people. Rather we saw two wonderful Christian people who were our dear friends personally and in Christ.

Two Hands Clasped

I was born and reared in the Deep South in the early years of this century. According to the social mores of the day in that area, whites and blacks each had and kept their *place*. I had never harmed a black person or been harmed by one.

During seminary days I was pastor of a church in Hope, Indiana. Only one black man lived in the town. One Sunday morning he was in the worship service. At the close, I was at the door shaking hands with the people. As the black man approached, thoughts were rushing through my mind. *I have never shaken a black man's hand in my life. What shall I do?* Then the thought came to me that in Indiana no such customary distinctions existed. So I shook hands with the man. To my surprise, his hand felt the same as others. I realized that it was a different custom, not Christian love, that had made the difference all these years.

Through the years of my life, Christian love has grown and been victorious. No longer do I see a black hand and a white hand. I see two hands of God's creation clasped in friendship and love.

A Portrait of Brotherly Love

In 1949 the Southern Baptist Convention met in Oklahoma City. The president was the late Dr. R. G. Lee. For the first time in the Convention's history, a black man from outside the fellowship was invited to preach. He was Dr. E. W. Perry, for over a half century pastor of the Tabernacle Baptist Church, Oklahoma City.

When Dr. Lee presented him, he put his arm about Dr. Perry and said, "Brethren, you are looking at a portrait of *black* and *white* painted in *red*" (see Eph. 2:13). The messengers stood and cheered.

Prejudice—A Universal Problem

Prejudice does not have a "Made in the U.S.A." label on it. Through the years as Frances and I traveled in other parts of the world, we found prejudice everywhere. For instance, in South America we found economic prejudice; in Europe, class; in India, caste; and in Africa, tribal prejudice.

While in Kumasi, Ghana, I heard that the superintendent of schools had made a trip to the United States to study the racial situation. He traveled from New York down the East Coast; across the deep South as far as Texas; through Oklahoma, Missouri, and the Midwest; then back to New York and his homeland.

Back in Kumasi he reported, "I find more prejudice in Kumasi than in the United States. There it is based on race; here is is based on tribal separation. For example, some say, 'I will teach your children in school, but I will not eat in your home.' Nevertheless, we are so much alike."

Do You Accept Others Socially

We may talk about not being prejudiced, but are we really? What does our witness say?

In Oklahoma City, one particularly fine Christian family, who lived in a lovely neighborhood, had a black family move next door.

They warmly welcomed their new neighbors. Not long thereafter the daughter of the white family was to be married. A group of friends gave her a bridal shower in the mother's home. The mother invited all her neighbors, including the black lady. Although she graciously declined to attend, the white family had given their Christian witness by their willingness to accept the black neighbor socially.

Guess Who the *Real* Foreigners Are?

Those who have traveled or resided in foreign lands know the loneliness and isolation resulting from differences in culture and language. "Yankee, Go Home" only adds to the hurt. Sometimes in our country one hears in references to some ethnic Americans, "Why don't they go back to where they came from?" Perhaps the American Indians feel that way about all of us.

In a humorous vein Will Rogers, who was part Indian, used to say, "Many people brag about their ancestors coming over on the Mayflower. My people went down to meet the boat!"

All One in Christ

In Miami Beach, Florida, in 1965, William R. Tolbert, Jr., an African, was elected president of the Baptist World Alliance by acclamation. The retiring president John Soren of Brazil said more Southern Baptists were present than all the other Baptists together. Such a large contingent of Southern Baptists could have elected anyone they wished. Nevertheless, without a dissenting vote the first African ever to hold this high position was elected.

Later, before more than sixteen thousand messengers, I pledged my support to Dr. Tolbert. I said, "I shake hands with many people, but I embrace only those I love. And I want to embrace Dr. Tolbert." As the multitude cheered, we embraced. I later learned that this was the way the African men show their love for each other.

Why did I embrace this black man? Not for acclaim. Not to show how broadminded or emancipated from prejudice I was. It was an expression of Christian love. For in Christ we were not *white* and *black*. *We were Christian brothers!*

CHARACTER

Fame is vapor; popularity an accident; riches takes wings. Only one thing endures, and that is character.
—Horace Greeley

J. P. Morgan was asked what he considered the best bank collateral. He replied, "Character."

Samuel Smiles reminds us that "to be worth anything character must be capable of standing firm upon its feet in the world of daily work, temptation and trial; and able to bear the wear and tear of actual life. Cloistered virtues do not count for much."

An open manner of life is a person's best safeguard against slander.

A Report of a Good Impression

Dr. John L. Hill, an employee of the Baptist Sunday School Board, visited an associational meeting in Southern Kentucky. He was deeply impressed by a young man who preached at the meeting. Years later Dr. Hill was approached by the pulpit committee of the First Baptist Church, Dallas, Texas, for a recommendation. He said, "Dr. W. A. Criswell is your man." At that time the committee had never heard of Dr. Criswell. But they followed up on this good report from a brother. Dr. Criswell's long ministry in Dallas confirms the value of both a good impression and a good report.

CHRISTIAN CITIZENSHIP/LIBERTY

No matter what theory of the origin of government you adopt, if you follow it out to its legitimate conclusion it will bring you face to face with the moral law.

—Henry van Dyke

Freedom is so beautiful a word that even if it did not exist one would have to believe in it.

—Goethe

The Christian and Government

Law-abiding people need have no fear of those who enforce the laws of the state. Instead, they are our protectors from wicked people. Only lawbreakers need to fear law enforcers. Unless you have broken the law, to see a police patrol car coming down your street should give you a sense of security rather than one of fear.

I must confess, however, that I once had a momentary scare. In the process of probating Mrs. Hobbs's will, I had to send a report to the Internal Revenue Service showing that no taxes were due on her estate. About three months had elapsed since sending it in, and I had not heard from them. On advice from my attorney, I wrote my congressman. A few days later I received a long distance call from Washington. When the caller identified himself as with the Internal Revenue Service, I instinctively asked myself, "Now, what have I done?" All he wanted was to tell me my report had been processed and approved. Naturally, I was relieved in more ways than one.

"For rulers are not a terror to good works, but to evil. Wilt thou then not be afraid of the power? do that which is good, and thou shalt have praise of the same" (Rom. 13:3).

George W. Truett on Religious Liberty

In his famous sermon on Baptists and religious liberty delivered from the Capitol steps in Washington, D.C., George W. Truett said, "There is a vast difference between toleration and liberty. Toleration is a concession; liberty is a right; toleration is a matter of expediency; liberty is a matter of principle; toleration is a grant of man; liberty is a gift of God."

Christians and Tyranny

While I was president of the Southern Baptist Convention, the Foreign Mission Board voted to give $35,000 toward rebuilding a Baptist church in Warsaw, Poland. The building had been bombed by American planes during World War II.

I received a letter from a Baptist man protesting this financial gift to "them Communists." I wrote back to tell him I knew some Polish and Russian Baptist leaders, and that they were very consecrated Christians. I also reminded the man that Christianity was born under the tyrannical Roman Empire and through the centuries had lived and labored under every form of government. Strong dedication is required to be a faithful Christian under a tyrannical form of government.

America—The Promised Land

Early one morning a group of us stood outside a hotel in Jerusalem. Around us gathered a group of Arab children, dirty and ill-clad. Their poverty and misery screamed at us. Most of the children begged for money. However, I will never forget the pleas of one little girl. "Please take me to America with you!" she cried. To her America was truly the "Promised Land."

Carving out a Nation

When our forefathers moved westward from the Atlantic seaboard, they carried an ax in one hand and a Bible in the other. With the ax they carved a civilization out of a wilderness. With the

Bible they laid the foundation of "one nation, under God."

Faith of Our Fathers

A nation is founded on and built out of the faith of those who bring it into being. A nation must be sustained by that same faith in forthcoming generations. When faith falters, the nation will not be far behind.

CHRISTIAN GROWTH

You cannot fight your battles in another person's armor.

Conversion Is the Beginning

Some years ago I was in the company of the late Gaines S. Dobbins at an assembly. During his long tenure as professor of religious education at Southern Baptist Theological Seminary, he exercised one of the greatest influences in our denomination. So he was qualified to speak out of great knowledge and experience. In his conference someone asked, "Is not conversion the end of evangelism?" Dr. Dobbins replied, "Yes. But which end?"

Why?

Most mothers of little children know how their patience can be tested by a child repeatedly asking, "Why?" Nevertheless, this question is part of the child's learning experience. Therefore, a wise parent will take time to give an explanation. If we honestly ask God "Why?" He will provide an answer. This will enable us to grow in spiritual maturity.

The "Bawl" Room

The late M. E. Dodd was one day showing a friend through his church plant. Finally, he said, "Now I want to show you our 'bawl' room." The friend was shocked to learn that they had a *ballroom* in the church. But he soon found himself looking at the nursery. Dr. Dodd laughingly said, "We just put the babies in here and let them 'bawl.' "

Too many Christians are in the "bawl" room when they ought to be pounding the pavements in search of souls for Christ.

Unlearning What We Know

A German mother asked a famous violin teacher to teach her son violin. He agreed. When she inquired as to the price, he said, "If someone else has taught him, the price will be $10.00 per lesson. If not, it will be $5.00 per lesson." Thinking this to be strange, the mother asked the reason for the difference. He said, "If someone else has taught him, I must first take that out of his mind. Then I will put in what I want him to know. If no other teacher has taught him, all I have to do is teach him what I want him to know."

Dr. A. T. Robertson's Testimony

Dr. A. T. Robertson was the greatest scholar of his time in the Greek New Testament. He wrote more than fifty scholarly books on the New Testament. His "Big Grammar," as he called it (1454 pages), was recognized worldwide as the classical work on the Greek New Testament.

His former students always will remember him as being hard on them. One day he said to me about his students, "They will be preaching the New Testament for the rest of their lives. And I want them to *know* it!"

He had a great passion for souls. His former students may find it hard to visualize him, during the invitation in a revival meeting, leaving the pulpit and walking up and down the aisles, exhorting lost people to receive Christ as their Savior. And many did so.

I sat in his senior Greek class at Southern Baptist Theological Seminary on a Monday afternoon in September, 1934. I was not more than fifteen feet from him, not knowing a stroke was coming on him that would take his life an hour and a half later.

On Friday before that he gave what was probably his greatest testimony about the New Testament. To our class he said, "Young gentlemen, I have been studying, teaching, preaching, and writing about the New Testament for more than fifty years. But I never open my Greek New Testament but that I see something I never saw before."

After his death a student received permission to take a picture of his desk just as he left it. I have a print of the picture. Dr. Robertson had been translating the Greek New Testament into English for a publisher. He had just finished Matthew's account of the feeding of the five thousand.

Papers and reference books were spread out on his desk. His pencil and the green eyeshades he wore when studying and writing were laying on the page on which he had been working..

In the midst of a busy task he laid down his pencil, took off his eyeshades, picked up his class books, and taught his class—and then went home and died.

Continuing to grow to the very end!

Toward the Horizon

Whether you travel by automobile or in an airplane, as you look ahead there is a limit to your vision. This point beyond which you cannot see is called the horizon. The horizon adds the element of adventure to your travels. It ever beckons you to discover what lies beyond. Through the ages the call of the horizon has caused explorers to venture into the unknown over land and sea. Intellectual horizons keep research scientists glued to their laboratories.

Spiritual horizons also beckon us onward. God's glory, love, and purposes have vistas that we have never seen. This fact causes the faithful to keep on keeping on. In faith we continue to travel toward the horizon of His will and purpose.

Take Time to Grow

When you come out of a river, you bring some of the river water with you. The water clings to you until enough time has passed to dry it up. Likewise, you come out of a worldly social order when you become a Christian. But some of the worldly ways cling to you. Time, instruction, and prayer are necessary for you to grow beyond such things into mature Christian character.

Roads Still Lie Ahead

Whether one be a new Christian, a babe in Christ, or a Christian who has sinned and found forgiveness, we must put a comma and not a period at the end of one's experience. The road of living for Christ still lies ahead. There are difficult hills to climb. Pitfalls await us. Dangers lurk on every hand. There are roaring streams to be crossed. Other crises, temptations, and trials are to be faced. So more than ever we need the Lord's help.

Don't Wait

One does not wait until he understands the principle of physical growth before eating or exercising. He does them knowing that beyond his comprehension growth takes place. The same should apply to spiritual growth. God has laid down certain conditions. The Christian should meet those conditions, and leave the results with God.

Marks on the Wall

Doubtless everyone remembers the times in childhood when he would back up to a wall so his mother might make a mark showing how tall he had grown. What a delight to find that the present mark was higher than previous ones!

This practice would be good for every Christian. He should measure his growth in grace and knowledge of Christ. This cannot be done by mere marks on the wall. But as one studies the character of Christ, he can examine his own life to see if he is growing more Christlike.

Public and Private Life

A person's public life is what he appears to be. His private life is what he is. Private immorality is practiced by immoral persons. The focus is on the difference between reputation and character. Reputation is what you do in the public spotlight. Character is what you do in the dark.

Real Beauty

Many years ago I met a lady whose outward appearance was practically devoid of beauty. But as I came to know her I witnessed character traits that sparkled like many diamonds. Through the years I have remembered her as one of the most beautiful persons I have ever known. That surely was what Paul had in mind when he wrote Colossians 3:12-14.

CHRISTIAN LIVING

Samuel Taylor Coleridge once commented: "Christianity is not a theory or speculation, but a life; not a philosophy of life, but a living presence."

In regeneration we are freed from the penalty of sin; in sanctification (dedicated service) we are freed from the power of sin; in glorification (reward and glory in heaven) we are freed from the presence of sin.

"Human things must be known to be loved; but Divine things must be loved to be known."
        —Blaise Pascal

It's not always so much *how* you do it but *what* you do that matters.

Christian people are not called to *fit in* but to *stand out*.

Before you can live as a kingdom citizen, you must be in the kingdom. This is possible only through faith in Jesus Christ the King.

Christian love does not ask, "Must I?" but "May I?"

I might have entered the ministry if certain clergymen I knew had not looked and acted so much like undertakers.
        —Oliver Wendell Holmes

It is not so much the power of positive thinking but the power of positive living that the world wants to see today.

Persons are to evidence a right relationship to God by the good things they do as well as by the bad that they do not do.

It is a sad day when the Lord's people choose to *stand in* the world, rather than to *stand out* for God in the world.

There Is a Difference

Someone asked William Barclay, the New Testament scholar, about a young man who described himself as a former student of Barclay's. Barclay replied, "He may have attended my lectures, but he was not one of my students."

How often this may be said of people who profess to be disciples (learners) of Jesus.

Christians Are to Be Different

William Barclay said: "Men need to discover the lost radiance of the Christian faith. In a worried world, the Christian should be the only man who remains serene. In a depressed world, the Christian should be the only man who remains full of the joy of life."

Reason for Doing Good

No person is justified in doing good simply on the grounds of expediency. To be sure, we should do good. Good deeds are to be done from a right motive as well as toward a proper goal. They are not be done to call attention to the person's goodness or piety but as an overflowing of God's goodness as He expresses it through His children.

You Did It to Me, Too

Jesus said, "Inasmuch as ye have done it unto one of the least of these my brethren, ye have done it unto me" (Matt. 25:40).

William Barclay relates two legends that illustrate this verse. These legends are not necessarily true in fact but are certainly true in spirit.

Francis of Assisi was wealthy, well-born, and high-spirited. He was unhappy, feeling that his life was incomplete. One day while riding on his horse, he met a leper—loathsome and repulsive in the ugliness of his disease. On an impulse Francis dismounted and flung his arms about the leper. Behold, in his arms the face of the leper changed into the face of Christ. Francis's life was never the same.

Martin of Tours was a Roman soldier and a Christian. On a cold winter day as he entered a city, a beggar stopped him and asked for alms. Martin had no money. Seeing the beggar blue and shivering from the cold, he took off his worn and frayed soldier's coat, cut it in two, and gave half of it to the beggar. That night in a dream, Martin looked into heaven where Jesus stood amidst all the angels. Jesus was wearing half of a Roman soldier's cloak!

Dig a Straight Canal

Have you ever looked down on a river while riding in a plane thousands of feet above the ground? If so, you know that the river's course winds here and there like the track of a large serpent. This is because in its formation the river followed the path of least resistance. On the other hand, a straight canal calls for advance planning, toil, and suffering as those who make it dig and blast their way through the terrain.

Lives are like that. Crooked or unrighteous lives follow the lines of least resistance. They twist and turn as they adapt to the changing mores of society. In doing so, they wander aimlessly with no certainty as to their final destination. Like those who dig a straight canal, the righteous determine their goal and pay the price necessary to achieve it. That is the way of Christ.

Armor or Cloak?

John Bunyan once said, "Religion is the best armor that a man can have, but it is the worst cloak." This striking statement distinguishes between religion that is simply skin deep and that which reaches down into the full depths of life.

Possess or Possessed?

We seek religion that is real rather than a sham. Charles Kingsley remarked, "What I want is not to possess religion but to have a religion that shall possess me."

Do You Qualify?

Many people define religion in terms of the negative rather than positive expressions. To them a good Christian is someone who does *not* do certain evil or questionable things. By this definition a clothing store mannequin could qualify, for it does not do any of those questionable things! Christianity should be seen as *positive* in nature. A true Christian *will* do certain good things because he or she *is* a Christian. A clean heart results in clean conduct.

An Eternal Investment

When a wealthy man died someone asked, "How much did he leave?" Another replied, "Every last cent of it."

"You can't take it with you" is a common expression. But you can send it on ahead! That's true whether we are talking about money, talents, opportunity, or time. The way to send it on ahead is to use it properly here on earth.

Jesus taught this truth in the parable of the unjust (or shrewd) steward (Luke 16:9). He also taught us to lay up treasures in heaven (Matt. 6:20). We may lay up treasures in heaven by investing our resources in those going to heaven: not in things but in persons.

The Enlightened Life

Helen Keller was physically blind but she saw infinitely more than most people with good eyesight who are blind in soul. She wrote:

Dark as my path may seem to others, I carry a magic light in my heart. Faith, the spiritual, strong searchlight, illumines the way, and although sinister doubts lurk in the shadow, I walk unafraid toward the Enchanted Wood where foliage is always green, where joy abides, where nightingales nest and sing, and where life and death are one in the presence of the Lord.

Jesus' Unique Golden Rule

Hillel, the Hebrew rabbi, said, "Do not do to thy neighbor what is hateful to thyself." Socrates, the Greek philosopher, said, "What stirs your anger when done to you by others, that do not do to others." Confucius, the Chinese sage, said, "What you do not want done to yourself, do not do to others."

These statements are worlds away from what Jesus said. Their rules are *negative* and *passive*. Jesus' rule is *positive* and *active*. In essence these wise men said, "Avoid doing to others what you do not want done to you." Jesus said, "Think of something good you wish someone would do for you, then do it for someone else."

Great Christian Living

A prominent Japanese Christian leader arrived in San Francisco for an extended lecture tour. A news reporter commented to the man that he had been referred to as "the greatest Christian in the world." The Japanese visitor responded, "I do not know who is the greatest Christian in God's sight. It may be a poor, unknown woman living in the slums of Tokyo." The man knew that in God's sight greatness is not determined by fame or the conditions under which one lives but by character and surrender to God's will and purpose.

The Key to Fruitful Living

One day we were flying from Cairo to Beirut. Due to hostilities the Arab plane could not fly over Israeli Mediterranean air space. We flew due east and then due north into Amman, Jordan. When we turned north, I went into the cockpit to take an aerial picture of the Dead Sea. On either side of the body of water as far as the eye could see, the land was barren. But running north and south was a narrow ribbon of green where the Jordan River flowed. The greenery never withered. The fruit trees, perhaps date palms, regularly bore fruit.

So it is with godly persons (see Ps. 1:3). Drinking from God's unfailing Word, they remain alive and prosperous. The promise is not necessarily to be understood in terms of material values. The Bible does not support a "name it and claim it" theology. However, persons who are rooted in God's Word discover the joy of living a rich, satisfying, and fruitful life. Something that is far more valuable than material things.

Christians Know the Difference

At the time of the 1937 flood in Louisville, Kentucky, I was pastor of a church on the outskirts of the city. Our community was the first stop to which the flood victims were brought. They came from all parts of the flooded area, and it was difficult to determine what kind of settings they had come from. Everyone was dirty from the ordeal, looking for a good meal and a place to sleep.

The next morning you could begin to distinguish some of the differences. Some of the people seemed content to remain dirty and unkept. Others were washing their hair and trying to spot clean their clothing.

I drew a spiritual lesson from this. People who do not know the better life that Christ gives are content to live in the dirt of the world. However, those who know what Christ gives seek to clean up their lives and live in accord with their new nature.

Some Guidelines for Christian Living

Here are four guidelines for living for the present while we wait for Jesus to come again:
1. Be discriminating in beliefs.
2. Be watchful.
3. Be loyal in telling the gospel.
4. Remain faithful in times of persecution.

The Moral Imperative

The people of our nation and the people of the whole world need to be gripped by the moral imperatives which grow out of the nature

of God, by a sense of right, by principles of truth, and by ideals of decency. Nothing is more needed by this sinful world than a revival of simple goodness and genuine uprightness.
—Clifton J. Allen

The Stewardship of Freedom

Charles Kingsley once wrote that "there are two freedoms—the false, where a man is free to do what he likes; the true, where a man is free to do what he ought." If we are to be truly free we must follow the latter, not the former.

Keep the Water Out of the Boat

For a ship to fulfill its purpose it must be in the water. But woe betide it if the water gets into the boat. Likewise, we are in the world. But we must ever be alert that the world does not get into us.

You Would Do Different

A man said to a preacher, "If I believed that I could be saved by grace without my good works, I would get saved and then have the time of my life doing what I want to do." The preacher replied, "Yes, you would have the time of your life doing what you want to do. But if you were really saved, what you would want to do would be far different from what you are now thinking."

Life in "Christ-control"

My automobile has the device called cruise control. On the highway I get the speed up to the legal limit. Then I push the cruise control button. With that I do not worry about the speed. Neither do I worry about the hills and valleys on the highway. When the car comes to a hill or mountain, the flow of gasoline increases automatically so that the car moves along at an even pace, regardless of the terrain.

In like fashion as a Christian I can move at an even pace along life's highway, whether the road leads through the even plains or over rugged mountains. When the going gets tough, I have strength for every challenge because of the One putting power in me. Regardless of what is happening around me, I know joy and peace within.

Why is this possible? Because somewhere along my Christian pilgrimage I put my life in *Christ-control.* Have you?

CHRISTMAS

That night when in Judean skies
The mystic star dispensed its light,
A blind man stirred him in his sleep,
And dreamed he had sight.

That night when shepherds heard the song
Of hosts angelic hovering near,
A deaf man stirred in slumber's spell
And dreamed him he could hear.

That night when in the cattle stall
Slept Child and Mother cheek by jowl,
A cripple turned his twisted limbs
And dreamed him he was whole.

That night when o'er the new-born Babe
The tender Mary rose to lean,
A loathsome leper smiled in sleep
And dreamed him he was clean.

That night when to his Mother's breast
The little King was held secure,
A harlot slept a happy sleep
And dreamed her she was pure.

That night when in the manger lay
The Sanctified who came to save,
A man moved in the sleep of death
And dreamed there was no grave.

—Susan M. Best, "The Miracle Dreams"

Light of the world so clear and bright,
Enter our homes this Christmas night;
Re-light our souls so tenderly,
That we may grow to be like Thee.
—Anonymous

What a Contrast!

What a humble birth! It is as though Christ *slipped* into the world—no fanfare, no king's palace, no silk-lined cradle. Just humble swaddling clothes and a manger with straw for a bed! From Rome, Caesar spoke and the world obeyed, yet for it all, he faded into an insignificant shadow in history. The world scarcely took note of Jesus' birth, yet the centuries have clothed him in glory such as the Caesars never knew. While the world hardly paused to note His birth, heaven bent low to herald to humble folk this event of the ages.

If Only It Could Last

World War I was characterized by trench warfare. Often the trenches of the two enemies were only a few yards apart.

I read a story in which the officers on both sides in one trench sector agreed that on Christmas Day they would permit the soldiers to come out of the trenches for Christmas fellowship. The troops gladly did so.

After a short time the officers order them back into their trenches. They realized that the soldiers could not fellowship together one day and then suddenly be enemies again.

The story reminded me of some words written many years ago. "Thus we can always know that men could live with goodwill and understanding for each other, because one day in each year the little Divine Prince of Peace still compels them to do it."

The Fullness of the Time

I recall reading a book by a Doctor Angus of Australia on *The Environment of Early Christianity*. After describing the environmental conditions in detail, he noted that by the end of the final century B.C. a fog of spiritual despair had settled over the civilized world. Humankind had tried every means available for salvation, only to end in despair. When they had reached the end of their tether of self-efforts to find salvation, that was *the fullness of the time*.

The Coming of the Baby

The birth of a new baby into a family is always a time of joyful celebration. It also is to be a time of reconsecration for the parents to the responsibility of rearing the child as God intends.

Even more so, for believers the world over Christmas is a time of rejoicing as we celebrate the birth of the Babe of Bethlehem. But it also is a heart-searching time as we commit ourselves anew to Him and to declaring the purpose for which He was born.

A Vision of the Eternal

In order to realize the true meaning of Christmas, you must look beyond the crib to the cross, from the Babe in a feeding trough to the Man on a tree, from the occupied manger to the empty tomb, yea, to the occupied throne. Thus Christmas becomes more than a day on a calendar. Christmas envisions eternal vistas—even eternal life for you.

What Is Christmas All About?

Christmas is more than tinsel and toys, trees and toddies, gifts and greetings. It is not merely a word of goodwill lightly spoken and soon forgotten in the raucous cries of conflict.

Christmas is a message of peace on earth among men who are pleasing to God. It is Immanuel, God with us. It is God bending low to lift men up out of the sin and mire of a world which has forgotten God and His will for lost men. It is God in a cradle, the Eternal in a tender baby's flesh and form.

But Christmas does not stop in Bethlehem. It reaches beyond to Calvary, to the empty tomb, and to the throne where the Savior sits, waiting for His enemies to become his footstool. It is the good news of salvation to all men who will receive it.

As the shepherds came to the manger, saw the Christ child, and went forth to tell the glad tidings; as the Wise Men came from afar to worship and give gifts to him, so should the faithful today bow before Him in worship, praise, and consecration; and then go forth to declare the gospel to a lost world. That is what Christmas is all about!

CHURCH/GOD'S PEOPLE

Every church should strive to be a little bit of heaven on earth. It should be a place where its people can find a haven of rest from the dog-eat-dog atmosphere of society where everyone is out to get *his*, regardless of what it does to others.

The theme song of some churches is: "As it was in the beginning, is now, and ever shall be, world without end. Amen. Amen."

God's People as Saints

God's people in the New Testament are identified as saints. The term refers to those who have been set aside in Christ. The emphasis is on *position* rather than *conduct*. However, *saints* are to act *saintly* in keeping with the holy character of God.

The Church and Human Need

A charge often hurled at churches is that they fail to come to grips with the human needs about them. This criticism should lead Christians to examine their concept of church life. The many activities within our church are not wrong unless they become an end unto themselves. Surely the primary purpose of a church's ministry is to meet humankind's spiritual need. But until a church has sought to meet the needs of the whole person it has not fully followed the example of Jesus. Efforts designed to meet the physical needs of lost persons can open doors to deeper spiritual ministry.

No Shrinking Violets

God's people are not to sit with folded hands waiting for their transfer to heaven. So long as they remain on earth there is work to do, battles to fight, and suffering to endure. Believers are not pictured in the New Testament as shrinking violets waiting to be plucked and carried into heaven. They are *slaves* of Christ who must be busy at his work. They are *soldiers* of Christ who stand in the fray as He battles against the forces of evil.

Not Everybody Does Church the Same

Since retiring from the pastorate I have been in churches all over the nation. Some are very informal in their worship service; others are more formal but not stilted. However, each kind is meeting the needs of the people to whom it ministers.

A pastor of a church on the eastern seaboard, now gone to be with the Lord, was one of the noblest Christians I ever knew. Some in the west regarded him as a *liberal*. He was not liberal in his theology, but in certain phases of ecclesiology he differed from his western brethren. I frequently checked the numerical results of his work to see if the criticism was warranted. Year after year his baptismal statistics exceeded the normal high. Liberal? No. He simply used methods adapted to the needs of the area where he ministered. Isn't that what Paul meant when he said, "I am made all things to all men, that I might by all means save some"? (1 Cor. 9:22).

A Church Is Missionary

I once heard a preacher, Jimmy Jones from Michigan, relate the struggles of his Detroit-area church. Faced with tremendous unemployment, decreased contributions, and ever-increasing utility bills, the church voted to decrease its giving to missions. One week later the church reversed its decision.

Jones told the listening group, "We learned that you can be a church and not pay your gas bill, and not have a building; but you can't be a church and not be missionary."

More Than a Building

Several years ago in Oklahoma City, a church decided to move to a new location. Once the *church* had built a new building, it sold the old one. With certain alterations the building became a restaurant. It was the same brick and mortar, steel and stone, but now it was used for a different purpose. Depending on the use made of it, a building may be filled with *hay* or *hosannas*.

The Church in the State

Certain things are clear from Jesus' words in Matthew 22:20-21. Church and state are not to be united. Neither is to control nor invade the domain of the other. Some of the darkest days in history are those where one dominated the other. Caesar's taxes should not be used in furthering the Lord's work. The Lord's tithes and offerings are not to be used for political purposes by either church or state. However, each has responsibilities to the other. The state should provide an orderly society in which the church can perform its mission. The church should produce the type of Christian character that is conducive to good government. In such a situation both church and state can realize their greatest potential.

Reviving God's People

If revival does not come within the church fellowship, it will not come anywhere! If revival does not come in us individually, it will not come in our churches. You can only *re-vive* those who have been *vived* in the first place. Revival does not mean to be saved all over again. Revival means that the fires of spiritual fervor, having become only hot embers, are again set burning with fervent, flaming heat.

Pattern of Church Divisions

Paul's comments to the church at Corinth (1 Cor. 1:11-12) can easily be applied to contemporary situations.

The Pauline crowd's loyalty was based on the past. They gave allegiance to the founding father instead of to their present leadership. They were as those who remain loyal to a former pastor, not the present one.

The champions of Apollos correspond to those who cling to a passing evangelist rather than to the pastor of the church.

The Petrine crowd suggest those who move from one church to another, but they do not transfer their loyalty to the new church and its pastor.

Like the Judaizers, certainly our primary loyalty ought to be to Christ, but we are not to make Him a part of church controversy.

Dealing with a Controversy

A friend sent me a cartoon showing an old man in a rocking chair. As he rocked, loud squeaks could be heard. After several futile attempts to get rid of the squeaks in the chair, the angry man got his shotgun and shot the chair into splinters. In the final frame of the cartoon, the old man is shown walking away, but the squeaks were still there. They were in his knees.

Sometimes the problems that exist in our church may be found within ourselves. Before we destroy everything else, perhaps we need to decide if we are part of the problem.

Church Problems Grow Larger, Not Smaller

As a boy on a farm I learned that you do not get rid of a stump by plowing around it. You remove it by digging it out or blasting it out with a power greater than your own.

Church problems are like the stump. You do not solve them by ignoring them. They will not grow smaller but larger. They are to be faced with courage and wisdom and in the power of the Holy Spirit.

How Churches Can Face Problems

When faced in prayer and dedication, problems from without the church tend to draw believers together. In such times as these the cause of Christ has known its greatest victories.

Look What You Can Get for Free

Many years ago in Oklahoma City a consulting psychologist spoke to the personnel directors of large companies. She said that people spend multiplied millions of dollars annually with psychiatrists for what they could receive in their churches for nothing.

Prince of Peace in the Church, Too

A quarreling Christian, church, or denomination is a denial of all for which the name of Christ stands. He is the *Prince of Peace*, not the author of strife. If Christians cannot live in peace with each other, who can?

Growing A Methodist Church the Baptist Way

One of the most rapidly growing churches in one southern city is a Methodist church that fifty years ago was drying up on the vine. Some Baptist pastors in town met with the Methodist pastor to learn the secret of the church's growth.

The pastor said they had taken a little book written many years ago by Arthur Flake on growing a Sunday School and followed his instructions to the letter. Flake called for community surveys, discovering new prospects, creating new classes and departments to which the prospects were assigned, and engaging in an intense visitation program to reach them.

Sounded good. The irony was that Arthur Flake was a Southern Baptist pioneer in building Sunday Schools and the book was published by the Southern Baptist Sunday School Board.

Here was a Methodist using Southern Baptist materials to run rings about his neighboring Baptist pastors in building the most dynamic and rapidly growing church in the city!

Church Life in Perspective

Churches are not to equate *bigness* with *greatness*—at either the local or convention level. Church organization is good when properly regarded, but woe betide us if we substitute *organization* for *organism*. Or mechanics for life! It is still "not by might, nor by power, but by my spirit, saith the Lord of hosts" (Zech. 4:6).

From a Little to a Lot

One Monday afternoon in a class Frances and I were attending as students at Howard College (now Samford University), the professor, Dr. L. O. Dawson, began class by saying, "Well, a little group of us met yesterday afternoon and organized a little Baptist church. We named it Edgewood Baptist Church. It isn't much now, but it will be a great church some day."

The church built its first building, a fieldstone structure, right in the middle of a woods in an area where few people lived. However, Birmingham was moving in that direction. Today the church is the Dawson Memorial Baptist Church, and it is one of the greatest churches in the Southern Baptist Convention. And thus the gospel spread. A little group of people saw a need, and they proceeded to meet it. Their efforts and His Word did not return void.

Wise Leadership

A wise leader, pastor or otherwise, will not approach a new task with the attitude that everything from the past must be removed in order to make a new beginning. The old is not bad because it is old. The new is not good because it is new. Indeed, the old may be better than the new. What worked in one place may not be successful in another. Before changes are made, time should be spent in evaluation. Furthermore, the people need time to develop confidence in the new leader. Sometimes the old adage is true, "If it ain't broke, don't fix it."

Supporting the Pastor

For ten years, which overlapped my pastoral-retirement years, I served as a trustee of Southern Baptist Theological Seminary. While still pastor, I was asked to serve as national co-chairman of a campaign to raise money to underwrite the Billy Graham Chair of Evangelism. A man in our church made a sizeable gift.

After I retired, I was asked again to serve as national co-chairman to raise ten million dollars for the seminary. Learning of it, this same man called me. He said: "Preacher, I hear you are leading another drive to raise money for Southern Seminary. I gave you a gift before, and I will help again. But I can't give anything like that amount, due to needs at our church. While you were my pastor, I supported you. Now we have a new pastor, and I am going to support him." Calling his name, I replied: "You certainly supported me all the way. And you are doing the right thing now in supporting your pastor." It should ever be thus.

COMMITMENT/CONSECRATION

God is not a doormat to be trodden underfoot at will.

During the Civil War someone is reported to have asked Abraham Lincoln, "Mr. President, do you think God is on our side?" He replied something like this, "My concern is whether or not we are on His side."

The world is still waiting to see what God can do with one person who is totally dedicated to His will.

A faith that is not worth dying for is hardly worth living for.

Sounds Like an Excuse

My first pastorate was the Vinesville Baptist Church, Birmingham, Alabama. Across the street from our church building lived a Baptist lady who was not a member of our fellowship. One day I visited her about it. She said she had not settled down and did not know how long she would live there. On inquiring, I discovered she already had lived there sixteen years. I had more brass and less sense then, so as I stood to leave, I said to her, "If you are not settled now, you won't be until they pat you in the face with a spade."

They Had the Right Idea

During World War II, I was pastor of the Emmanuel Baptist Church, Alexandria, Louisiana. At that time a natural gas pipeline was being laid from South Texas to the East. One Sunday a couple joined our church by letter. Later he told me they would only be with us about six weeks. He added, "I am helping to lay the pipeline. We are constantly on the move, but we want to have an active church life. We look ahead to find a church within reasonable driving distance and join it. When we get too far beyond it, we look ahead to find another church." They had the right idea.

It Pays

A teenage boy made a profession of faith. After the service, his Sunday School teacher said to the pastor, "As you know, I have had many problems with him. At times, my heart ached over what seemed to be a hopeless task. What happened here this morning more than repays me for all the trouble through which I have passed." Such satisfaction cannot be measured in monetary values. Furthermore, they inspire us anew to behold our God.

Such Determination

Dr. A. T. Robertson related this instance from the life of Martin Luther as he faced the challenge of the Diet of Worms: "Spalatin begged Luther not to go on. Luther said, 'Though devils be as many in Worms as tiles upon the roofs, yet thither I go.' "

A Paraphrase of Luke 9:62

If you look back only to the road over which you have just come, your car will become a pile of junk metal.

Keep Your Eyes on the Ball

In football a player is told that to catch a pass he literally is to *look* the ball into his hands. Otherwise what might have been a touchdown and victory will be nothing more than an incomplete pass.

Jesus calls us to follow Him. We gain the victory by keeping our eyes on Him.

The Test Is in the Life

Billy Graham held a one-month crusade in Oklahoma City in 1956. In 1983 he was back in the city for a one-week crusade.

Someone asked me if the results of Dr. Graham's crusades really lasted. My reply was that a man who was saved in the 1956 crusade was the general chairman of the 1983 crusade. I could tell of many similar cases.

The test of any crusade or revival meeting is not determined at its conclusion. The test is in the ongoing commitment expressed in the lives of those who were spiritually touched.

Questionable Commitment

A businessman and a minister were traveling by plane in a terrible storm. The minister overheard the businessman pray, "Lord, if you will get me safely through this, I will give You half of everything I own."

When the plane landed safely, the minister encouraged the businessman to fulfill his promise to God. The man replied, "Preacher, I made the Lord an even better deal. I told Him that if He ever caught me on a plane again, I'd give Him *everything* I own.

No Less

One of the greatest sayings in military history came from British Admiral Horatio Nelson, "England expects every man to do his duty." Thus, in the midst of one battle he cried, "Westminster Abbey or victory!" In other words, "Death with honor—victory!" If nations expect that kind of commitment from its citizens, should we give any less to God?

Look What God Can Do with a Committed Person

God often raises up his champions in the most unlikely places. A carousing baseball player—Billy Sunday—became the outstanding evangelist of his era. A shoe salesman who could not even speak good grammar—Dwight L. Moody—inflamed America and Europe with his evangelistic fervor. God plucked A. T. Robertson, one of the greatest of New Testament scholars, and George W. Truett, one of the outstanding pulpiteers of the Christian era, from the mountains of North Carolina.

God still goes to out-of-the-way places to find many who serve Him mightily. God can use anyone who is wholly dedicated to His will! He can use you!

Shallow Commitment

A woman had taught a Sunday School class for years. One day she told her pastor she was resigning. When he asked her reason for doing so, she said, "Someone has criticized my teaching." Although it had never happened before, after one carping criticism the lady was ready to throw in the towel.

Crawl or Fly?

In his first sermon to the church a new pastor said, "This church has been crawling. If I am to be your pastor, it has got to walk." The people said, "Amen!"

Then he said, "If I am to be your pastor, this church has got to run." The people said, "Amen!" He continued, "If I am to be your pastor this church has got to fly." Again, the people shouted, "Amen! Amen!"

Continuing the pastor said, "And if this church is going to fly, it will take a lot of hard work and money." To which the people said, "Uh, Oh! Let it crawl!"

Default Leads to Repossession

In buying an automobile, you make a down payment. Then you sign a contract drawn up by the dealer or financing institution. The contract stipulates that you must make installment payments at stated times until you have completed payments on the car. So long as you do so, you keep and use the vehicle. If you default on the payments, the dealer or lender may repossess the car. He is bound by the promise that you are able to keep the car as long as you meet the stated payments.

What if you had such a covenant with God? Would you be in danger of default?

Be True to Christ

George W. Truett was one of the greatest preachers in Christian history. Yet in the closing months of his life he suffered beyond measure from the disease that took his life in 1944. Though in his condition he had sought to resign his pastorate of the First Baptist Church, Dallas, Texas, the church refused to permit it. That forty-seven-year relationship was dissolved only in death.

Not long before Dr. Truett's death, arrangements were made for him to preach his last sermon to his congregation by telephone from his bed. As the people listened over loudspeakers placed in the church auditorium, not one word of complaint over his lot did they hear. The repeated refrain was "Be true to Christ!"

COMPASSION

This day in honor I have toiled;
My shining crest is still unsoiled;
But on the mile I leave behind
Is one who says that I was kind.

—Anonymous

An Incentive for Preaching the Gospel

Many years ago Frances and I made a missionary tour around the world. Though government regulation at that time prevented Southern Baptists from having mission work in India, we spent some time in that country.

Arriving in Calcutta at 2:30 in the morning, we were driven to the hotel by our driver. The climate of India is semitropical, but as we drove through the business section we saw what looked like snow covering the sidewalks. Closer examination revealed that people dressed in white were sleeping on the sidewalks.

Frances questioned the driver. He said the owners of the stores paid them to sleep there to guard their stores. I accepted his answer at face value, but not Frances. She saw poverty beyond description everywhere. Later as we were on our way back to the airport she continued to probe about the *sidewalk people*. Finally, the driver admitted they had no other place to sleep. He said that millions of Indian people live out their lives without ever having a roof over their heads or ever having a full stomach.

We later learned that their hunger problem was directly related to their religion. It was a spiritual-economic problem. This became an added incentive for preaching the gospel of Christ to them.

Compassion at Work

God wants us to care for those in need. We are to share with them what we have, whether it be clothing or food—two of life's necessities. Simply to feel sorry for such people is not enough. Where it is within our ability to do so, we should meet their needs.

In Houston, Texas, where my son and his family live, a local television station sponsored a "Feed the Poor" event. Early in the morning an announcement was made that people could bring food to a certain location on a busy thoroughfare. Early morning traffic was tremendously heavy. Shortly before noon the station ran pictures showing drivers handing sacks and boxes of food to the eager hands of volunteers standing on the curb. They received tons of food. Many gave checks. The news report showed pictures of both happy givers and receivers. I am convinced the Lord was happiest of all.

The Grace of Understanding

After several pastors had failed to win a condemned criminal to Christ by *preaching down* to him, a layman went to visit the man. Entering the death row cell, he sat on the cot alongside the man, took him by the hand, and said, "We are in a bad fix, aren't we?" The man broke into tears and soon yielded to Christ. He needed somebody to understand and care.

Weeping for Souls

Many times tears are effective where reason fails. C. E. Matthews was a warm-hearted, evangelistic preacher. He told me of an experience he had during a revival meeting. In the community was a lost man who had resisted the efforts of many preachers to win him to Christ. One evening just before the revival service Brother Matthews and the pastor sat in a car with the man. He had sought to reach the lost man by explaining the plan of salvation to him, but to no avail. Finally Brother Matthews burst into tears. That broke the man's resistance. He received Christ as his Savior and later that evening made his public profession of faith. Where reason had failed, tears for his soul prevailed. Have you wept over a lost soul lately?

CONFESSION

The Supreme Question

When I attended the seminary the custom at exam time was for the professor to write out the questions with the grade value of each written in parentheses. Mimeographed copies were given to the students. On one New Testament exam Dr. A. T. Robertson gave only two questions. The first question had a value of twenty. The second was valued at eighty. Obviously, the latter question was of greater importance.

Jesus gives an exam that has only one question. That question has a value of one hundred. Everything depends on the answer. The question is, "Who do you say that I am?"

An Unexpected Confession

At an evangelism conference, one preacher invited, "I realize that this congregation is mostly composed of preachers and their wives. But there still might be an unsaved person. I feel led to give an invitation for you to accept Christ. We sang an invitation hymn and much to our joyful amazement, a man came from the balcony to make his decision. He was dressed in his work clothes and related this story.

"I am a cross-country truck driver. Passing through Birmingham, I saw this church. Seeing this crowd, I decided to park my truck and come in. As I listened to this man's sermon I was convicted of my sins. I have repented of them and have given my heart to Jesus. I am so thankful that I had this opportunity to make that decision public before you."

CONVERSION

It's What's Inside that Counts

"Clothes make the man"—or woman—so a popular saying goes. But do they? Scoundrels may be dressed in the best fashion, but they are still scoundrels. Conversely saints may be clad in rags, but they are still saints. The clothes *on* the person is not what counts but who is *in* the clothes.

He Called Me Brother

As a boy he had been kicked, cuffed, and cursed by unloving parents. He developed a hostility toward life and people. The world retaliated in kind. As a man he knew no friends. He had been called everything base and mean under the sun.

Hearing about him, a Christian man went to visit him. In response to a knock the man opened the door and snarled, "What do you want?" The visitor replied, "My brother, I have come to visit with you." When the visitor departed, he left behind a changed man, a Christian. Later an acquaintance, noticing the difference in the man's life, asked, "What brought about the change?" The man replied, "He called me *brother!*"

What a Turn Around

Billy Sunday was reared in a Christian home. Later he fell in with the wrong crowd. One night he attended a mission service and was gloriously saved. He went on to become one of the great evangelists of the century.

CONVICTION

A faith that is not worth dying for is hardly worth living for.

Courage consists not in blindly overlooking danger, but in seeing and conquering it.
—Jean Paul Richter

> Cowards die many times before their deaths;
> The valiant never taste death but once.

—Shakespeare, *Julius Caesar*, 1.3

Taking a Stand

During the War Between the States, Rebel and Union soldiers were in a skirmish near a home. As they were shooting at one another, an aged grandmother picked up her broom and started toward them. Someone called for her to come back, that she could do no good with a broom. She replied, "I can at least show 'em which side I'm on!"

The Best "Man" Was a Woman with Convictions

In the United States in the early 1950s, a crisis arose when Senator Joseph McCarthy made widespread claims of Communist infiltration into all areas of American life. In the hysteria that followed, many lives were ruined, the ranks of foreign diplomats were decimated, and charges of Communist leanings were made against numerous high officials, including the president. No Republican of national stature would challenge Senator McCarthy, not even the president. Finally, Republican Senator Margaret Chase Smith, the only woman in the Senate, rose to present a scathing 'declaration of conscience' condemning Senator McCarthy for his irresponsible tactics. In 1954 the Senate passed a censure motion that brought the crisis under control. It began because one woman dared to speak her convictions.

Loss with Gain

Polycarp, bishop of Smyrna, died a martyr's death about A.D. 155. A mob demanded his death, but the Roman officials sought to spare him. Arriving in the arena of execution, the proconsul urged him to revile Christ and save his own life. Polycarp replied, "Eighty and six years have I served Him and He hath done me no wrong. How then can I speak evil of my King who has saved me?" For this Polycarp was put to death. For his conviction he lost his physical life, but he gained life eternal.

He Took the Risk

A few years ago in midwinter, an Air Florida jetliner bound from Washington, D. C., to Tampa crashed into the Potomac River. One woman struggled hopelessly for her life in the icy waters. Suddenly a man in the crowd dived into the cold river and brought her to safety. He risked his life to save a woman he had never seen and did not know. One moment he was "Mr. Anonymous," just an ordinary guy. The next moment he was a hero.

What made him do it? He did not know himself. Nevertheless, the moment of crisis brought out the best and deepest convictions in him.

COOPERATION

It takes many trees to make a forest and many grains of sand to make a seashore.

Harmony in God's Will

In the sixty years of my ministry I have noted that religious controversy, whether in a local church or in a denomination, usually is between people or groups that sincerely believe they are doing God's will. Often I have said that in every disagreement there are three sides: yours, mine, and the right one. Where religious matters are involved the *right* one is God's side. A proper resolving of the problem comes only when contending parties find and accept God's side or do His will.

Cooperative Though Independent

I once heard W. A. Criswell describe our denomination as "a bunch of speckled birds." Of course, he spoke in jest. But he aptly described us. The very nature of our church polity invites or allows for differences among us. I have often said that we are an independent people who express our independence through voluntary cooperation.

One but Different

Some neighbors were discussing the different outlooks people have. Finally, one old man said, "Well, I am glad all people don't see alike. Because if they did, they would all want my Marthy." These neighbors were one in community but recognized their differences. So it is to be in the body of Christ.

The Conductor Knows

An orchestra has many instruments ranging all the way from tubas and drums to fifes and piccolos. Each instrument is important. The harmonious blending of their sound results in symphony.

Let's suppose that the piccolo said, "With all these other instruments making so much sound, no one ever hears me. So when it's my turn, I will not play." The audience would likely still enjoy the music, but the conductor, alert to every sound, would know the piccolo did not play.

Likewise, if you refuse to use your gift, however small, in a cooperative effort, Jesus will know and the work of the church will not be complete.

All Three Count

Imagine an old farmer using a mule to plow a field. In a tree on the edge of the field a mockingbird sings. There's no glamor in the work, none in pulling the plow, and no practical substance in the song of the mockingbird. However, both the mule and the bird have a role in the farmer's life. The mule is essential to preparing the soil to bear a harvest. The bird's music adds joy to the farmer's toil. And in the end, all three may share in the fruit of the harvest.

We Were Co-Laborers

When I became pastor of the Dauphin Way Baptist Church, Mobile, Alabama, it was my privilege and responsibility to follow Dr. C. B. Arendall, a great pastor and wise leader. He had exercised that role for twenty-one years and was dearly loved by the people.

Before preaching my first sermon as pastor I paid tribute to Dr. Arendall and his family. In doing so I said: "My family and I have not come to take their place, but to make ours alongside theirs. We do not want you to love them less because we are here. Indeed, if after twenty-one years you did not love them, we would be afraid of you. Your continuing love for them proves your capacity to love us."

This statement came from my heart, but is was also good strategy. The people were set at ease regarding my relationship with Dr. Arendall. Their hearts were joined with ours as we became "laborers together with God" (1 Cor. 3:9). Dr. Arendall lived only fourteen months after this, but he was my strongest supporter until then. As long as I was in Mobile his wife, until her death, and family, including two deacon sons, continued this support.

Talking Themselves Together

Through sixty years of working with my denomination I have learned that if you let them talk together long enough, either they will talk themselves together or else in good spirit accept the outcome even when they vote differently. When we fail to talk to one another or do not allow ample opportunity for discussion we run into trouble.

A Baptist came home from a church business meeting. His wife, who did not attend, asked how things went. He replied, "Great! It was one of the best business meetings we ever had. I made three speeches myself!"

All for One, One for All

The wagon trains of the Old West for the most part were made up of strangers bent upon one goal—to seize the opportunities offered by the broad expanses of the West. As people traveled together they became acquaintances and then friends. Normally, the train of wagons stretched out one behind the other; in a sense each was on its own. But if attacked by enemies, the wagons formed a cohesive circle to give greater strength and safety. It was all for one and one for all.

Due to the dangers which assail us, Christians should be united in the circle of divine love. If they are, then no combination of evil forces can destroy them.

Unity and Uniformity

We must distinguish between *unity* and *uniformity*. The former is voluntary; the latter is compelled. The former is an inner condition; the latter is outward form. Unity must be the condition created in us by the Holy Spirit as we follow him in a common goal and purpose—to make effective God's redeeming work in Christ to the ends of the earth and until he comes again.

DEATH

The young *may* die; the old *must* die. Death will come unless the Lord comes first.

God's Grace Is Sufficient Even in Death

On September 27, 1984, Frances, my beloved wife of fifty-seven and one-half years went to be with the Lord. A few days prior to that I conducted the funeral service for Dr. Henry L. Lyon, Jr., a retired Baptist pastor, whose dear wife, Louise, was Frances's sister. He was my brother-in-law for over fifty-five years.

A few months later I preached the sermon at the funeral of Lillian Grey, the beloved wife of Dr. J. D. Grey. For almost forty-four years the Greys and the Hobbses were bosom friends.

All three couples—Hobbs, Lyons, Greys—lived well beyond our Golden Wedding Anniversaries. When death came to our spouses, we, along with our families and friends, grieved because of our losses. But in our grief we sense the light of God's love shining through our tears, making a rainbow of promise in our souls.

The three surviving spouses know what we have preached and taught by faith for almost sixty years. *God's grace is sufficient!* Our departed loved ones are "absent from the body . . . present with the Lord" (2 Cor. 5:8). Whether the Lord comes or tarries, before long we too will be reunited with these loved ones and with all God's children. There, forever we will praise the triune God for His atoning love and grace.

Going to a New Home

Not to grieve would be less than human. As Christians, however, our grief is more for ourselves than for believing loved ones who die. We know they are far better off (see 2 Cor. 5:1,8; Phil. 1:21,23). We have been left behind and are lonely.

Think it thus. You and a loved one live in a rundown section of a city. A time comes when the loved one's *house* is no longer fit for human habitation. By some good fortune he/she inherits a beautiful mansion in the elite community of the city. You rejoice because of the new home, but you grieve for yourself because you are left behind and are lonely. Infinitely so this is what death means for Christians.

A Thoroughfare to the Father

Death is not a blind alley, but a thoroughfare into the Father's "House of Many Mansions." Death is not a box canyon with only one way in and no way out. Death is a pass through the mountain into the beautiful green valley of eternal fellowship with the Lord and with loved ones gone before.

Facing Death

When I knew that my wife, Frances, was terminally ill, I wrote to tell Billy Graham about it. He replied with a long letter of comfort. But as long as I live I will never forget one statement he made. He wrote, "I long for heaven, but I dread getting out of this old body."

That is the natural feeling of every faithful Christian. Paul himself in essence said the same thing in Philippians 1:21-23.

No Fear of Death

Mrs. Hobbs never expressed fear of death. Knowing that she faced possibly great suffering, she said to me, "I hope it will not be long." God spared her the worst of that. On one occasion after I had ministered to her, she said, "I am sorry to put you through this!" I assured her it was a ministry of love.

Two things were of major concern to her. One was for me. She asked our children and her sister, "Take care of Herschel!" The other was for her sister's husband who was having health problems. Finally, Frances went to sleep in the Lord in our bedroom and woke up in the Fathers *House of Many Mansions*. The Christian need have no fear of death!

Grief at Death

Through the years I have noticed that the ones who have the hardest time handling bereavement are those who are unwilling to accept that a loved one has died. When a person accepts the fact of death, he or she is able to face the future as it will be.

When Frances went to be with the Lord, people remarked how well I handled it. My answer was that when I knew she was terminally ill, I said to the Lord, "Fifty-seven and a half years ago you gave her to me. Now I am giving her back to you. Do with her as you will." I found peace in the will of God.

This did not mean that I did not want to keep her. Oh no! But if keeping her meant ever-growing pain for her in order to satisfy my own selfish desires, no! I loved her too much for that.

Grief is natural. I know, for I have grieved—and continue to do so. But my grief is for myself. I know Frances is far better off with the Lord, but I am left behind and lonely.

Differences in Grief

One day I stood with two brothers before the casket of their deceased mother. She had lived with one of the sons, who gave her tender, loving care until her final breath. His emotions ran deep. However, he shed no tear, made no cry, but only looked at her body.

The other son had lived far from his mother, seldom visiting or even writing her. He came only when told that his mother was near death. His emotions ran near the surface. As he viewed his mother his loud crying could be heard a block away. Both his emotional nature and his neglect of her entered into his strong, outward demonstration.

Both brothers grieved, but in such different manners—due largely to background and emotional make-up.

Songs in the Night

Charles Haddon Spurgeon preached a sermon on "Songs in the Night" (see Job 35:10). He gave reasons why we should sing in the night. One was that others who travel the same dark way will hear, find guidance, and receive strength. So in your night of bereavement—sing! Sing for your own welfare and for that of others. In so doing you will find help for the *night* and assurance for the *day* that soon will dawn.

Magnifying Christ in Death

When Dr. Louie D. Newton died at the age of 94, he was the oldest living former president of the Southern Baptist Convention, a position I used to occupy. Someone told me how he died. His family was all gathered about his bed. They all joined in prayer. Then they sang "Amazing Grace." As soon as that was finished this grand old soldier of the cross smiled—and then quit breathing. He magnified Christ in death as in life.

A Picture: "And That Is Death"

I stand upon the seashore. A ship at my side spreads her white sails to the morning breeze and moves softly out to the blue ocean. She is an object of beauty and strength. I stand and look at her until at length she hangs like a speck of white cloud just where the sea and sky come down to mingle with one another.

Then someone at my side exclaims, "Look, she's gone!"

Gone where? Gone from my sight, that is all. She is just as large in mast and hull as she ever was. Her diminished size lies in me, not her. And at the very moment when someone at my side exclaims, "Look, she's gone!" there are other eyes eagerly watching her approach, and other voices ready to take up the glad shout, "Look, she's coming home!"

And that is death.

—Anonymous

DECISION/FREE CHOICE

Today is God's day; *tomorrow* is the devil's day.

Inherent in being a human being is the privilege of free choice. Had God created us otherwise, we would be nothing more than puppets on a string of fatalism.

Both God and Satan are looking for *tools* to use. Whose tools will you become?

Before Christ there is no neutral ground.

Once You Hear, You Must Decide

A person cannot hear the gospel and not be responsible for the reaction given to it. To receive the gospel brings life; to reject it brings spiritual death.

The Importance of Decision

Someone said there is a point in the Rocky Mountains where raindrops fall ever so close together. However, those falling on one side of the ridge flow westward toward the Pacific Ocean; those falling on the other side of the ridge flow southeastward toward the Gulf of Mexico. The raindrops fall so near each other, but wind up so far apart.

This may be an apt illustration of people making decisions for Christ. Persons may be in the same family or social group. Yet their decisions for or against Christ determine whether their eternal destiny is heaven or hell. At the moment the difference may seem so slight. But destinies are bound up in the decisions they make. Persons are to ponder long in deciding about so vital a matter.

Who Is to Blame?

If a person knows that the bridge over a canyon is gone, he erects warning signs along the road leading to it. But a motorist sees and ignores the signs. As a last resort the concerned person stands in the road earnestly trying to stop the motorist from certain tragedy. Still the motorist ignores the warnings, runs down the person giving the warning, and plunges to his own death. Who is to blame? The answer is obvious.

This parallels what God has done in Christ to save people from hell. Those who reject His efforts to save are to assume responsibility for the results, not God. God does not *send* people to hell. They *choose* to go there! God only *permits* it when every overture of his saving love is rejected.

The Ball Is in Your Court

I don't know a lot about tennis. However, I do know that sometimes "the ball is in your court." That means that the opponent has returned the tennis ball back across the net and onto your side of the court. What happens at this point in the game is up to you. Either you can stroke the ball back across the net, or you can let the ball go by you and lose points in the game. The decision is yours.

Love Is a Two-way Street

A college student returned to his dormitory room crestfallen and despondent. His roommate asked what was wrong. The young man said, "I asked my girlfriend to marry me and she turned me down." His roommate replied, "Well, cheer up! You know a woman's 'no' really means 'yes.' The despondent young man answered, "But she did not say 'no.' She said, 'Aw phooey!' "

Love is a two way street. Offered love requires a response. When God offers His love, we can accept it or reject it.

As You Will

Some boys liked to taunt a wise old man. One day they brought the man a little bird that was held tightly in one boy's hands. They asked the man to tell them if the bird was dead or alive. Knowing that the bird was alive, but that with a squeeze of his hands the boy could instantly kill the bird, the old man said, "As you will, my son! As you will."

As to the kind of persons we will be and the type of world we will have, God says, "As you will, My child. As you will."

Mercy or Justice?

Jeremy Taylor once said, "Mercy is like the rainbow which God hath set in the clouds: it never shines after it is night. If we refuse mercy here, we shall have justice in eternity."

Losing Your Chance to Respond

Psychologists say that if you refuse to respond to a stimulus, in time the stimulus goes away. The stimulus may return, but it is usually weaker than before. After several occurrences, the stimulus ceases or else the person becomes hardened and unable to feel it. Thus the person loses the ability to respond positively.

So it is with the convicting power of the Holy Spirit. Persons may reject the Spirit until they become so insensitive that they do not/cannot respond positively.

The Best Argument-Experience

A lost man said to a Christian witness, "If you will tell me who Cain's wife was, I will become a Christian." (As if this had anything to do with salvation!) The witness replied, "She was Mrs. Cain. Now let us get on with the business."

As a means of avoiding a decision many lost people want to debate issues, even what is necessary to be saved. A clever debater may be able to refute your logic, but no one can deny your personal experience with Christ.

A Mixed Response

So often people give different responses to the same thing. Three people view a masterpiece in art. One exults in its beauty, another examines the workmanship, and the third is bored with the entire matter. Two people hear the same sermon. One is convicted of his sin, believes in Jesus, and is saved. The other hardens his heart, rejects Christ, and is lost.

DRUNKENNESS
ALCOHOL

One of the best social arguments against the use of alcohol is in the words of Lady Nancy Astor: "When I have a good time, I want to know about it."

Drink has drained more blood,
Hung more crepe
. . . .
Broken more hearts,
Blasted more lives,
Driven more (to) suicide, and
Dug more graves
    than any other poison scourge that ever swept
    its death-dealing waves across the world.
        —Evangeline Booth

General Robert E. Lee is said never to have promoted a man who drank alcohol. His reason? "I cannot consent to place in the control of others one who cannot control himself."

The saloon is a cancer on humanity, eating at its vitals and threatening its destruction.
        —Abraham Lincoln

My medical experience has taught me that the effect of alcohol is temporary, evanescent; that the drug does no real good, and that a dangerous habit is thus easily engendered which may be most difficult to eradicate, a habit which may utterly ruin the patient—body, soul, and spirit, making it far better if he had died at once of his disease while under the doctor's care.
        —Dr. Howard Kelly

All my life I have lived in the presence of fine and beautiful men,

going to their death through alcohol. I call it the greatest trap that life has set for the feet of genius.
—Upton Sinclair

Nothing can make a monkey into a human being. However, alcohol (or other drugs) can make a human being act like a monkey—or worse.

The one who clasps the bottle to his bosom as he would a cherished friend might just as well clasp a rattlesnake.

The Truth of the Matter

A few years ago billboards across the nation advertised hard liquor by featuring "The Man of Distinction." Truth in advertising should have required another billboard featuring a human derelict called "The Man of Extinction." That is the true end of the alcohol road for millions of its victims.

The Christian Ideal

We talk about *temperance*, but the Christian ideal is *total abstinence*. If we would be true to the highest and holiest within us through the indwelling and power-filling Spirit, total abstinence is not merely an ideal. It is the only practice for a Christian!

The Stewardship of Influence

A young man was killed in an automobile accident while driving under the influence of alcohol. His grief-stricken father raged against whoever sold his minor son the alcoholic beverages. He demanded that the police find and punish the man! Imagine the father's compounded grief when he opened his own liquor cabinet to find the following note from his deceased son: "Dad, I took a bottle of your liquor. I hope you don't mind."

A Tragedy That Could Have Been Avoided

In my college pastorate an alcoholic made a profession of faith. He became very active in church work, but he insisted on continuing his association with his drinking friends. I begged him not to do it. He insisted he wanted to prove to them he could resist drinking. Soon he was drinking again.

One afternoon he came home is a drunken rage. His wife was absolutely true to him, but he accused her of unfaithfulness. He threatened her with a gun. Just as he started to pull the trigger his eleven-year-old son ran between them and took the bullet in the stomach. Thinking he had killed his son, the man ran into the garage and took his own life. His son recovered, but the whole tragedy could have been avoided had the man avoided alcohol.

The Happy Hour

Many places that furnish public accommodations, such as hotels and motels, each evening have what they call "The Happy Hour." It is merely an euphemism for "The Cocktail Hour." Its purpose is to enable people by means of alcohol to escape temporarily from a drab, humdrum routine for a brief *happiness*. Alcohol lowers a person's inhibitions. For a time it enables him/her to open up and mingle freely with others. But after a time alcohol depresses. So when the effects of the alcohol are gone, nothing has changed. The awareness of the unhappy happenings returns.

In this light we understand in part Paul's words in Ephesians 5:18. "And be not drunk with wine, wherein is excess, but be filled with the Spirit." Instead of getting a temporary lift from alcohol, have the permanent glow of personality through the indwelling Holy Spirit.

EVANGELISM/WITNESSING

Some want to live within the sound
Of Church or Chapel bell;
I want to run a rescue shop
Within a yard of hell.
                    —C.T. Studd

The Christian's responsibility is not to *win* but to *witness*.

In witnessing, "I know" is better than "I think."

If an indifferent Christian could spend just five minutes in hell, he would come forth as a flaming evangelist seeking the lost.

In evangelism the contents of the message and the method of presenting it are to adhere to the highest standard of integrity.

Too often we *gossip* the bad things and ignore the good things. Christians need to *gossip the gospel*.

The difference between evangelism and missions is largely one of geography.

The harvest is at our doorstep as well as in fields across the ocean.

We have the only remedy for the world's ills. What a shame that we share it in dribbles when we should do so in a flood.

A Good Question

The Duke of Wellington is best known for his defeat of Napoleon at Waterloo. However, one time a young minister asked him for advice as to how he could succeed in the ministry. The Duke asked, "What are your marching orders?" The young man quoted

85

the Great Commission in Matthew 28:19-20. The Duke responded, "Then what are you waiting for?"

Just Sow the Seed

A farmer does not wrest the plant from the seed. He sows the
seed and leaves the result to God. If God's people are faithful in
sowing the seed, God will be faithful in giving the harvest.

Anytime, Any Place

For the Samaritan woman (John 4) the wayside well became a
cathedral in which Jesus could present His claims to a needy soul.
From Him we learn that the Christian can witness anytime, any
place. We cannot allow those opportunities to slip away.

A True Success

The greatest obstacle for witnessing is the fear of failing. Persons who witness cannot fail. The very act of bearing witness is
success!

Adjectives or Verbs?

I was talking with a friend about a statement another friend had
written. He said, "I think it is a beautiful statement. I like the
adjectives he uses, but I also want to see more *verbs*." As you know
adjectives are descriptive words; verbs are action words.

The same may be said about our discussion of concern for the
lost. We can speak of it with glowing adjectives. But we need to
demonstrate our concern with verbs. We need to do something
about it by putting our concern into action.

You Are Salt

As a farm boy, I recall that when we butchered a hog my mother salted down the meat by rubbing salt into it. This prevented it
from spoiling. The salt was applied to the meat but did not become
a part of it.

As Christians are salt, they must be in the world, but they are not to become identical with its evil system. We are to be witnesses to the saving power of Jesus Christ. Jesus said more about being a witness than about witnessing. We are to bear our witness to the lost. Unless we are a witness by what we are, our bearing a witness will be but empty words.

Numbers May Not Count

We have become slaves to numbers in judging the lasting effects of our evangelistic efforts. In Scotland only one little boy was saved in a revival. That was Robert Moffatt, the missionary! In North Carolina, in two revivals only one boy was saved in each. One was A. T. Robertson, who later became one of the greatest New Testament Greek scholars; the other was George W. Truett, who became the "prince of preachers" among Southern Baptists!

But Just Suppose . . .

If a person took a dollar and doubled the succeeding amounts twenty-one times, he would have $1,048,576. This illustrates what could happen in evangelism. If one person won another, and both of them won someone the next day—and if this practice were continued by all—in twenty-one days 1,048,576 persons would be led to Christ.

Impractical? Jesus would not say so. That was His goal. Think what a different world this would be if His disciples through the ages had followed this plan!

Just suppose that the fourteen million Southern Baptists should engage in this kind of witnessing for a year. Just suppose the pastors would do this. Just suppose the members of one Sunday School class should do this. Just suppose . . . ?

Get to Know Him Better

One way to get to know Jesus better is to tell someone else about Him. Telling your Christian experience deepens and freshens it.

Gathering the Fruit

When I began my ministry, the pattern was for churches to have an annual two-week revival. Many people were saved, others came into the church fellowship by letter, and members were revived. The emphasis was on how many joined the church. At the end of the year we found that most new members came during the time of the annual revival meeting.

Today we emphasize evangelism week by week throughout the year. We reach far more people this way. The approach may be likened to gathering ripened fruit that falls off the tree at the slightest shaking of the limb. We gather the fruit Sunday by Sunday rather than waiting to harvest it all at once. Under this plan more people are absorbed more effectively into the church fellowship.

Our Silence May Haunt Us

The famed German pastor, Martin Niemoeller, said:

"In Germany, the Nazis first came for the Communists, and I didn't speak up because I wasn't a Communist. They came for the Jews, and I didn't speak up because I wasn't a Jew. Then they came for the trade unionists, and I didn't speak up because I wasn't a trade unionist. They came for the Catholics, and I didn't speak up because I was a Protestant. Then they came for me, and by that time there was no one left to speak for me."

Do You Really Believe It?

A man was condemned to be hanged for his crimes. A pastor went to see him in an effort to lead him to Christ. He spoke to the condemned man about his lost condition and fate. He told him about Christ's redeeming love and work to save him. After listening, the condemned man said, "Preacher, do you really believe all this?" The preacher affirmed that he did. "Well, preacher, do all Christians believe this?" Again the preacher said they did. To which the man replied, "Well, I don't believe it. But if I did, I would crawl on my hands and knees across this city to tell someone about it."

Friend or Fiend?

If God should reveal to someone the cure for cancer and that person kept it a secret from all other people, we would regard the person as a fiend. How else should both God and others regard us if we have God's revealed cure for a far more terrible malady, sin, but we refuse to share it with those lost in sin?

Witnessing Like Jesus

Missionary E. Stanley Jones asked Indian leader Mohandas K. Gandhi what Christians could do to win India to the Christian faith. He replied that the Christians should identify with people as Christ did during His time.

Too Busy Having Fun

Suppose you were on a cruise ship in the Caribbean. Suddenly on one side of the boat are hundreds of people in small boats that are sinking. The people cry out for help. If they are not rescued soon, they will drown. What should you do?

Then you hear the captain of the ship announce over the speaker system: "Folks, look to the other side of the boat so you won't see those people. Put your fingers in your ears and you won't hear them. Oh, they need help, but after all, this is a pleasure cruise, not a rescue mission. We are too busy having fun. Oh, yes. You can say a little prayer for them as we pass by."

Criminal? Yes! But no more so than when we ignore the cry for help by people all about us who are being swallowed in an ocean of evil. Too many believers are too busy to help "rescue the perishing." They are too busy enjoying their—of all things—religion!

Jesus Expected Nothing Less

In Matthew 28:19 "go" often is translated as an imperative form of the verb. In reality the word form is a participle, meaning "going" or "as you go."

The meaning is like a wife speaking to her husband who is on his way to the store. She does not say, "Go to the store and get me a spool of thread." He already is going to the store. So she says, "Since you are going to the store will you bring me a spool of thread?"

Thus Jesus said, "Since you are going." He never for one moment entertained the idea that with such a glorious message of salvation His friends would not go and share it. We certainly should do no less!

He Holds Us Responsible

Suppose you have a Japanese neighbor. Someone asks you, "If you were a missionary in Japan, would you try to lead Japanese people to Christ?" Of course you would reply, "Yes!" Then the rejoinder comes, "Have you tried to lead your Japanese neighbor to Christ?" How would you answer?

God does not hold us responsible for opportunities we do not have. However, He does hold us responsible for the one we do have.

Persistent Sowers

During the drought conditions a few years ago, much of the seed that had been planted did not come up. The seed that did produced runty plants that promised a scanty yield, if any at all. Grass burned up in the intense heat, and the cattle nearly starved. Many farmers were forced to sell their cattle.

Except those who faced bankruptcy or foreclosure, few farmers were giving up. In many cases they could be seen plowing up hopelessly lost crops and planting other seed. They worked in hopes of refreshing rain and an eventual harvest.

If they were so persistent, should sowers of the seed of the Word of God do less? Yes, many will reject our witness. Others will receive it superficially, only to show their true colors when the going gets rough. Some will truly be saved but will yield little or no harvest as they get caught up in the temporal things of this age. But we must persist, knowing that others will be saved and will give themselves wholeheartedly to the service of the Lord, yielding an abundance of souls led to Christ (see Mark 4:1-20).

A Strange Letter

Recently I received a strange letter from a person with whom I was not acquainted. It came from a state far removed from Oklahoma. The writer had recently been saved, and sent a blank certificate of ordination to the ministry, requesting that I ordain this person to the ministry. The letter expressed the writer's strong desire to go everywhere telling people about the Lord's great salvation. It also revealed this person needed much doctrinal training.

Of course, I returned the certificate. I pointed out I did not have the authority to ordain anyone. I added that the church of which this person was a member or else one that knew the person should tend to ordination. I concluded that one could bear witness to the Lord without being ordained.

I also thought what a glorious thing it would be if every Christian possessed the enthusiasm expressed in this letter. Even so, to be most effective such people need to be taught the way of the Lord "more perfectly" (Acts 18:26). It is the responsibility of the churches to do this teaching.

You Knew When He Was Around

The late Robert G. Lee was fond of saying of Paul: "Wherever he went, he started either a riot or a revival. Put him in jail, and he would come out with the jail door under one arm and a convert under the other."

FAITHFULNESS

The Son of God goes forth to war,
A kingly crown to gain;
His blood-red banner streams afar.
Who follows in His train?
Who best can drink His cup of woe,
Triumphant over pain;
Who, patient, bears his cross below,
He follows in His train.

....

A noble army, men and boys,
The matron and the maid,
Around the Saviour's throne rejoice,
In robes of light arrayed:
They climbed the steep ascent of heav'n
Through peril, toil, and pain;
O God, to us may grace be giv'n
To follow in their train.

—Reginald Heber

At times it may seem that God's way is slower. But it is sure. Happy and wise beyond measure are those who, without wavering, walk in it.

There are no crown-wearers in heaven that were not cross-bearers here below.
—Charles Haddon Spurgeon

God is not in the business of growing hothouse orchids, but sturdy oaks which have endured triumphantly the storms of the years.

The soldier of the cross who falters and retreats in the face of the enemy is not worthy of the name he bears.

Jesus Cheers the Faithful

Acts 7:55 notes that Jesus was "standing on the right hand of God" as Stephen's enemies stoned him to death. Why was He standing?

Let us suppose you are a football fan. The score is tied with less than a minute to play. Your team has the ball on the opponent's one yard line. What would you be doing? Sitting down? Reading the player's names on the program? Idly twiddling your thumbs? No! You would be standing, cheering for your team to score!

So Jesus cheers for those, like Stephen, who are faithful unto death. What looks like defeat to some is eternal victory.

God Favors Faithfulness

Some one has said that in war Providence is on the side of the strongest regiments. And I have noted that Providence is on the side of clear heads and honest hearts; and whenever a man walks faithfully in the ways that God has marked out for him, Providence, as the Christian says—luck, as the heathen says—will be on that man's side. In the long run you will find that God's Providence is in favor of those who keep His laws, and against those that break them.
—Henry Ward Beecher

What a Compliment

I was asked to conduct the funeral of a former aide to former Governor "Alfalfa Bill" Murray. Prior to his death the aide had asked the governor to bring the eulogy. Governor Murray had occupied the office during a rather stormy period in the state. By this time he was an aged man confined to a wheelchair. However, his voice remained strong. During the eulogy he boomed one word repeatedly in reference to his deceased aid—loyalty. Through all the tumultuous period this aide had been faithful. That is what God seeks and expects from those who would serve him.

Don't Play for the Crowd

Ben Chapman and I were fellow students in Phillips High School, Birmingham, Alabama. Ben became a professional baseball player and played as an outfielder for the New York Yankees along with Babe Ruth. Later he managed a big league club.

After his first season with the Yankees, Ben visited Frances and me. I asked, "Ben, how do you like being a big league ballplayer?" He answered, "I like it fine. The salary is good. The only thing I don't like is that with the crowd you are a hero today and a bum tomorrow."

However, as a true athlete Ben was not playing to the crowd, but doing his best for the manager.

In the Christian game of life we are to be willing to pay the price for standing by our convictions. We are not to play to the crowd. Instead we are to be "looking unto Jesus the author (pioneer) and finisher (goal) of our faith" (Heb. 12:2). His "well done" drowns out the raucous jeers of the fickle crowd.

Thomas Carlyle on "Duty"

Let him who gropes painfully in darkness of uncertain light and prays vehemently that the dawn may ripen into the day, lay this precept well to heart: Do the duty which lieth nearest to thee, which thou knowest to be a duty. Thy second duty will already have become clearer.

Riding for the Brand

Over the years of my life I have enjoyed reading stories of western lore. Out of this reading have come two sayings: "Riding for the Brand" and "He'll do to go to the well with." The former meant that a cowboy was loyal to the owner or "brand" for which he rode. The latter grew out of custom. When the early settlers expected an attack by Indians or outlaws, they would gather at one place in order to pool their fire power. Food and water were stored in the cabin or ranch house. If the siege was prolonged they often would run short on water. One man would be selected to go to the well for water. In turn, he chose the man he trusted most to go along and guard him. Hence the saying "He'll do to go to the well with."

Servants of Christ should ride for His *brand*. They should be so trustworthy that other Christians would trust them with their very lives.

FAMILY/HOME

A house is built of logs and stone,
Of tiles and posts and piers;
A home is built of loving deeds
That stand a thousand years.

—Victor Hugo

Faith in each other binds the family together.

Neglect in giving religious instruction to children is to invite moral and spiritual disaster.

Charles Haddon Spurgeon, speaking of children and parental discipline, said, "If we never have headaches through rebuking them, we shall have plenty of heartaches when they grow up."

The happy family is but an earlier heaven.
—Sir John Bowring

The Importance of a Godly Home

Arthur A. Hicks puts the home in proper focus:

No church, nation, or civilization rises higher than the spirit of religious reverence and worship that prevails in the home life of its people. The home that is not genuinely Christian is not a true home. It is God's first institution of human society and is the ultimate basis of society. It is the citadel of both church and state which so nobly serves our social order.

When the Shoe Is on the Other Foot

Reaching back over the years I recall a popular song that belonged to a more nostalgic age. Its title was "Baby Your Mother

Like She Babied You." In less romantic terms, the song reminded us that the time comes when the shoe is on the other foot. We seldom hear such songs anymore. But its message still speaks to us. Just ask yourself one question. *How would it have been with you had your parents treated you then as you treat them now?*

Honoring Parents

One of the most heartwarming commercials on television pictured a mother in tears. When asked why, she said to her husband, "Our son called (long distance) today." Her husband asked if anything was wrong. When she replied in the negative, he inquired, "Well, why are you crying? Why did he call?" Smiling through her tears, she answered, "He said, 'I just called to tell you that I love you, Mom.' "

Jesus honored His mother. If we would fully follow Him we must do the same for our parents.

No Greater Obligation

In simpler bygone days when a child was born, a family simply planted a few more rows of food. In a few years another farm-hand would be available. Now, however, a child is an economic liability rather than an economic asset. The birth of a child creates a financial obligation for parents. The greatest obligation, however, is that of rearing a child in the will and way of the Lord.

A Child's Faith Is Like a Rosebud

Frances and I had many rose bushes in our backyard. Each spring they put out their leaves, and eventually rosebuds appeared. Ere long they became beautiful blossoms. One of my jobs was to cut roses for the home. If I cut one while the bud was still tight, it never opened. If I got them just as they began to open, they became beautiful blossoms in the home.

Children are like that. We must watch for that moment when their hearts begin to open to the overture of the Spirit, then seize that opportune moment. Thus they become beautiful blossoms ever enlarging to gladden the heart of God.

What Constitutes a Family?

A family is not simply a group of people dwelling under one roof. By that definition any hotel or prison could qualify. A family is not a group of people bearing the same name. Persons with the same name may live all over the nation and be total strangers.

A family can have a variety of compositions—parents and children, a married couple without children, a single parent and children, among others. Family is not simply people but a spirit of oneness. It is a spirit produced through loving and longing, laughter and tears, shared joy and sorrow, mutual struggle and respect, faith and joy and sorrow, mutual struggle and respect, faith and faithfulness, and a common pursuit of worthy goals.

Notice the Difference

Carpenters, masons, electricians, and plumbers can build you a house. Only you and yours can build a home.

The By-products Are Valuable, Too

While in college Frances and I studied pandemic chemistry. On a field trip to a coke factory we were told that for untold years the smoke from coal burned in industry simply escaped through smoke stacks into the air. Then it was discovered that the smoke contained many by-products, some far more valuable than the coal itself. So manufacturers began burning the coal in a manner that would conserve the smoke. In this process by-products like coke, an excellent fuel, were produced.

Certain by-products come from the application of Christian principles to the home. Obeying one's parents produces the by-products that contribute to the longevity of the nation. Children who learn discipline and respect in the home under the tender care of loving parents are unlikely to have a need to be taught those qualities by the strong arm of the law.

Importance of a Good Beginning

Someone said, "As a rule, a person will continue in the way he starts in childhood. This truth is especially evident in a child's self-image and the pattern of his relationships with other persons. This is the time to lay the foundations for a right relation with God and other persons."

The Family Wants Your Best Side, Too

In public we are on our best behavior. It is within the walls of the home that our religious profession finds its greatest test. Such a love will avoid the harsh words spoken in a fit of anger. We regret them as soon as they are spoken. They probably will be forgiven, but they leave their scars. It is far better to endure the pressures of family living with sweet reasonableness than to strike out with harsh words that may serve only to compound the problem.

The Necessity of Cultivation

The same fertile soil will grow weeds or profitable plants. If left to itself, a piece of land will become a wilderness of weeds. To produce a profitable harvest calls for preparing the soil, planting proper seed, and constant cultivation.

Children are like that. If parents want to produce something other than weeds, they must pay the price in toil and care. It may seem to be the harder way, but it is the proper way.

Give the Child a Chance

Whenever a baby is born, in essence God says, "Take this child and rear him or her for me." The tragedy is that so many babies are more *damned* than *born* into the world. They are unwanted, uncared-for—left to grow up like weeds in a wilderness. Fortunate is the child and wise the parents when the parents seek and follow the guidance and will of the Lord in rearing their child.

Unlimited Potential

I have lived to see babies grow up to become presidents of the United States or heads of other governments. Who knows but that a child in your home, even your unborn or yet unconceived child, may be the one chosen to lead the world out of its morass of confusion, misery, and trouble. We should follow God's guidance in rearing them in the event He chooses to use them to that end.

We Did Our Best

Through the years I have counseled with godly parents whose children did not turn out to be all they and the Lord wanted them to be. Invariably the parents asked, "Where did we fail in rearing our child?" All the while I knew they had done all that parents could do to rear the child in the fear and admonition of the Lord.

My reply was always as follows:

> You did your best. But there comes a time when they encounter influences contrary to your teaching. We have our children for such a short time. All that we can do is teach them the will and way of the Lord, lead them to have faith in Him, and instill in them principles of righteous living that will strengthen and guide them in the choices they must make. And then pray for them. Both parents and children must be willing to follow God's guidance.

I have often quoted a statement by Dr. George W. Truett. It will bear repeating here: "To know the will of God is the greatest knowledge. To do the will of God is the greatest achievement. The will of God is not always easy, but it is always right."

These words are *timeless* in their import. They are *timely* for you and me.

FORGIVENESS
RECONCILIATION

A person should drown the hatred of others in an ocean of love.

Loving One's Enemies

One of the greatest tests of the degree of a person's transformation into the likeness of Christ is his reaction to the one who does evil to him.

One in God's Amazing Grace

One Sunday many years ago I was part of a touring party in Cairo, Egypt. We were strangers in a strange land. We were separated from the nationals by language, dress, culture, and different economic and political systems. Furthermore, we were Christians; they were Muslims. All day we had heard the people talk with one another, but not one word did we understand.

That evening in a little Baptist church we were welcomed, not as American tourists, but as fellow Christians. The first song we sang was "Amazing Grace." They sang in Arabic; we sang in English. Overriding it all was our mutual love for Christ and for one another. Truly God in Christ had made of two one new people.

How to Destroy Your Enemies

A king said, "Today, I shall destroy all my enemies." At evening they were still living. When asked about this, the king said, "I *have* destroyed my enemies. By doing good to them I have made them my friends."

Respect for a Foe

During the Civil War someone reported to Abraham Lincoln that one of his contentious cabinet members had referred to him as a fool. Mr. Lincoln replied, "Well, I must check into that, for I have found that he is usually correct in his judgments."

Heap Coals of Fire

A woman brought suit against her husband for divorce. She told the judge she had nagged and nagged the man but he just wouldn't do right. Referring to Paul's words in Romans 12:20, the judge asked the woman if she had tried to "heap coals of fire on his head." The woman answered, "No, but I don't think it will work. I've already tried scalding water, and that didn't do any good."

Do We Have to Forget to Forgive?

We sometimes hear, "I cannot forgive if I cannot forget." This idea is born of the devil. If we ever really know something, we never forget it. While a wrong done to us may still be in our minds, however, it need not be in our hearts. This means that we do not continue to hold in our hearts the wrong done to us. If God has put our sins behind us, we can do the same with the sins others commit against us. Because of His infinite love, mercy, and grace, God chooses in Christ to regard our sins as never having existed. We can do the same if we have the will to do so. We can regard the sins committed against us as never having existed. Failure at this point robs us of joy and usefulness in our Christian lives.

Hearts That Beat as One

Did it ever occur to you that God has put rhythm in everything that He created? One sees it in stars and atoms, in seasons and harvests, in the beauty of a flower and in the song of a bird. The surf of the sea, the majesty of a mountain, and the beat of the human heart say that God has put all nature in tune. When they get out of tune, trouble results.

If rhythm is in natural things, why not in human relationships? They also are the Creator's design. Only when persons get out of tune does strife erupt.

Before every concert the orchestra tunes itself to one basic tone. Otherwise, the result would be cacophony and not symphony. Only as men tune their hearts to God's heart of love will they be reconciled to Him and to each other.

Why We Can Forgive

God expressed His love for us through Christ. He covered our sins in Him. Thus, through faith in Jesus we are reconciled to God. In that light surely we should be willing to cover sins done to us by other people. Not that we can forgive sin on God's behalf, but we can do so in our relations to others.

Responding to a Wrong

The English word *reconcile* comes from the Latin *re*, again, *conciliare*, to unite. Between people it means to restore friendship.

Let us suppose you have wronged a friend. This mars the friendship. Lovingly the friend offers to wipe the slate clean. However, friendship is a two-way street. If in your stubborn will you refuse to admit your wrong and accept forgiveness, the friendship is marred the more. In effect you have said to the other person that you do not want his or her friendship. But if you respond positively to the offer, the things that separate you are removed. You are reunited; or in the Greek sense, you exchange your wrong for the other person's forgiveness, so that you are reconciled.

FUTURE LIFE

Intimations of Immortality

Apart even from biblical truth, there is in the soul of human beings the intimation of immortality. We see it in such diverse places as the burial customs of the Egyptian pharaohs and of the American Indians. Provisions for life after death were interred with them.

Our modern scientific age is no exception. Charles Darwin said, "To those who fully admit the immortality of the human soul, the destruction of our world will not appear so dreadful."

Sir James Young Simpson is more to the point. "It is simple dogmatism that would deny immortality; on scientific grounds, at any rate, we have not the knowledge to take up such an attitude."

Sir William Osler states it strongly: "In the presence of so many mysteries which have been unveiled, in the presence of so many yet unsolved, the scientific student cannot be dogmatic and deny the possibility of a future state . . . of the things that are unseen science knows nothing, and at present has no means of knowing anything."

Louis Pasteur, at the bedside of his dying daughter, said, "I know only scientifically determined truth, but I am going to believe what I want to believe, what I cannot help but believe—I expect to meet this dear child in another world."

Is there beyond the silent night
An endless day?
The tongueless secret locked in fate
We do not know—
We hope and wait.

Looking for Proof

Some time ago a magazine that deals with the sensational carried a headline: "Proof That There Is a Future Life!" The story reported cases of people who seemingly had died, but returned to life to describe what they had experienced. As I read the headline I thought that no such evidence was necessary for "proof." For thousands of years the sublime truth has been taught in the Bible.

Blessedness in the Christian's Death

Often people grieve because someone died and was deprived of certain earthly blessings: a recent retiree who never lived to enjoy a well-earned leisure; a young person who died before achieving certain goals in life. But this is to look at only one side of the picture, and the lesser one at that. For "Blessed are the dead which die in the Lord from henceforth: Yea, saith the Spirit, that they may rest from their labours; and their works follow them" (Rev. 14:13).

I'll See You in the Morning

I delivered the eulogy at the funeral of Ramsey Pollard, one of my dearest friends among preachers. After recalling his sterling qualities and recounting some of the good times we had together, I closed by saying, "Good night, Ramsey. I'll see you in the morning!" Yes, it's "good night here, but good morning up there."

Suffering of Hell

Charles Howard was one of the most ardent evangelists I ever knew. One time I heard him preach on hell. He said that one of the greatest sufferings of hell will be remembrance of lost opportunities to believe in Christ as Savior (see Luke 16:25-26).

GIVING/STEWARDSHIP
TITHING

Only when we discover the *grace of giving* do we experience the *joy of living.*

Someone said the most sensitive nerve of humanity is the *pocketbook* nerve.

Giving Won't Kill You

A pastor spoke to the deacons about a proposed missionary offering. One deacon objected, saying, "Pastor, if you don't stop talking so much to our people about giving money, you are going to kill this church!" The pastor replied, "I don't think so. I have never heard of anybody or a church giving itself to death. But if that should happen, I am going to conduct the funeral. I will stand on the front steps of the church building and read loudly, Revelation 14:13—'Blessed are the dead which die in the Lord'!"

Give Until It Feels Good

An oft-used slogan is, "Give until it hurts." It does not take much giving to hurt some people. Instead, we should "Give until it feels good." Years ago a deacon told me about his experience in tithing. "The first time I did it, it seemed like all the money in the world. Now I look forward to payday, so I can give my tithe and more."

Reason for Stewardship

Instead of needing our gifts, God gives us the things necessary for life—life itself, breath, and every material thing. True, the Bible teaches the stewardship of life and substance. However, God is not within Himself dependent on such. Stewardship is designed to develop His people, whose very gifts are a recognition that all belongs to Him and comes from Him.

Life's Supreme Obligation

A man was asked why he did not tithe. He replied it was because he owed so many people. When reminded that he also had a debt to God, he said, "Yes, but He isn't pushing me like the others are."

This would be humorous if it were not such a serious matter. The fact is God does press His claims upon people. He does not violate a person's will by coercion, but no one can ignore His claims with impunity.

Begin with the Little

A great philanthropist was asked how and when he learned to tithe. He replied, "By tithing my first week's salary of $2.50." Few people learn to tithe the *much* if first they have not learned to tithe the *little*.

Tithing and the Ancients

Many years ago I read a tract written by Dr. J. E. Dillard. He was once my pastor at Southside Baptist Church, Birmingham, Alabama, and later the promoter of stewardship with our denomination's executive committee. In the tract Dr. Dillard noted that whereas ancient peoples have been found who did not practice animal sacrifice, none have been found who did not have the tithe as the basis of giving to their gods or God.

The Tithe Is Reasonable

Although it is not the Christian standard and certainly is an unworthy motive, even if you put tithing solely on a business basis, it makes good sense. Invest a dime and get back ninety cents. That's quite an investment.

Tithing as the Beginning

In the Bible the tithe is not the goal. It is the beginning. The Old Testament speaks of tithes *and* offerings. New Testament steward-ship includes *all* that we have and are.

More Than a Financial Plan

Someone said that tithes and offerings are not simply God's plan for financing His work. Primarily it is a means by which the Lord develops His people. Giving is an acknowledgment that all we have and are belongs to God. What we possess has been entrusted to us to use for His glory. As His stewards we *own* nothing but are *responsible* for everything.

Inspired Giving

A pastor wrote the president of a seminary to inform him about a man in his church who was capable of giving the school $50,000. The president invited the man to visit the campus. After showing his guest around the campus, relating what the seminary was doing, and feeding him a sumptuous meal, the president took the man to his office to attempt to *sell* the man on the idea of giving a donation.

On the way they met a professor of preaching who was a personal friend of the potential donor. After a brief chat the man asked the professor what he would do if he was able to make a gift to the seminary. The professor said he would give $500,000 to endow a chair of preaching.

The president cringed, fearing the professor had ruined everything he had been trying to do. He was right! The man did not donate $50,000. Instead, he gave the seminary $500,000. He had been inspired to give.

Preparation for Giving

My predecessor at Emmanuel Baptist Church, Alexandria, Louisiana, was Kearnie Keegan. While he was pastor there, a young banker was asked to lead the Every Member Canvass. The traditional method had been to announce a Sunday when the church would begin receiving pledges. Canvassers worked for a month soliciting pledges from the church members. When the month was over many members were angry over being asked to pledge, only about eighty-five percent of the budget was pledged, and the canvassers quit their solicitation with the hope that the rest of the money would come in.

The young banker asked himself, "Why not spend a month preaching on stewardship and preparing publicity and mailouts? Then pledge the entire budget in one day?"

Thus began a revolution in the stewardship program of that church. It worked! The month ended with victory and a church family rejoiced in it. The success of the program could be seen from year to year by noting the increased budget goals that were established.

When I became the pastor, I began sharing the idea with my pastor friends, who also used it successfully. I carried the idea with me to Dauphin Way and First, Oklahoma City. It always succeeded.

The plan succeeded because the people's minds and spirits had been prepared for giving to support the church's plan of ministry. They had been inspired to give! A worthy goal with proper preparation will produce an ample, joyful response.

Opposing a Pledge to Give

Some people excuse themselves by saying they do not believe in pledging. However, they pledge when they buy a car or house on time payments. Any credit buying is a pledge. The only difference between that and a church pledge is that in the business world failure to meet the obligation results in losing the purchased item or being taken into court. Some people strain out gnats and swallow camels. We can be certain that God knows the true reason for failure to give to His work—rebellion against Him.

A Ready Response

In the late 1930s many churches were considering building programs. They hesitated because times were uncertain, the economy was unstable, and war clouds hovered over Europe. Hitler's invasion of Poland and subsequent declarations of war in Europe only added to the problem. Inevitably the United States would become involved, so many people believed wisdom necessitated putting their building programs on hold.

During this same period of time, different things were happening in the Dauphin Way Baptist Church, Mobile, Alabama. Under the dynamic leadership of my predecessor, Dr. Charles B. Arendall (whom one deacon called "A Steam Engine in Britches"), and the faithful "followship" of the people, the church went ahead with its plans to build a large auditorium and other facilities. Plans were drawn, contracts were let, and all building materials were purchased and delivered.

Construction began in 1940 and the building was completed in 1942. The project was paid for by December, 1944. I succeeded Dr. Arendall on January 1, 1945, entering a beautiful, commodious church building *debt free*.

The Widow's Mite

Mrs. Windsor was a dear, sweet little lady about ninety-five years old. In her younger years she was active in all phases of church life. For years she lived about a block from the church, never missing a service, even though it was difficult for her to attend.

Finally, she went to live in a nursing home, which prevented her from attending the church. However, every time anyone from the church visited her she asked the person to take her offering to the church.

A deacon visited her during the time the church was engaged in a renovation program costing hundreds of thousands of dollars. Mrs. Windsor said to him, "I read in the church paper that they are fixing up the church buildings. I will never be able to attend again, but I want to have a part." So she gave him a dollar bill.

The deacon returned to the church and with tears in his eyes, he told me the story. Then he said, "Pastor, this dollar bill is sacred. It is truly the 'Widow's Mite.' I am turning in one of my dollars in its place. I want to have this one framed and placed with the story in the Fountain Room" (a central gathering place in the building).

Long since, the deacon and Mrs. Windsor have gone to be with the Lord, but that dollar bill still bears witness to a dedicated handmaiden of the Lord who had a generous heart.

Giving with Purpose

A wealthy lady in our church gave vast sums to the Lord's work through our church. When she died, her granddaughter thanked Frances and me for what we had done for her grandmother. She said, "You added ten years to her life by giving her a purpose for living." Such blessings are not reserved only for the wealthy stewards. They accrue to anyone who sows bountifully according to his or her ability to do so.

The Nature of Stewardship

Charles Simmons said, "As to all we have and are, we are but stewards of the Most High God. On all our possessions—our time and talents and influence and property, He has written 'occupy till I come.' To obey His instruction and serve him faithfully is the true test of obedience and discipleship."

Giving in Perspective

Although I never made it a practice to inspect the giving records of the people, one year our church business manager showed me the amount a wealthy man had given. The total was an unusually large amount even for a wealthy man. So the next time I saw him, I commended him for it. He said, "Pastor, I do not deserve any credit for giving. During the year my wife and I wanted for nothing. In fact I gave her a new fine car, and we took a trip to

Europe. I made no sacrifice like some. If you must hand out a commendation, give it to some poor person who gave out of great sacrifice."

You've Got It All Wrong

During a stewardship preparation period a pastor preached several consecutive Sundays on giving. One member commented, "I'll be so glad when the pastor quits preaching on money and gets back to preaching the gospel!" I have never heard a good steward say that. Giving is part of the gospel.

Generous to a Point

One man asked another, "If you had a thousand hogs, would you give me half of them?" "Sure!" came the man's rely. "Well, if you had a hundred hogs, would you give me half of them?" Again, "Sure!" was the answer. "Okay, if you had two hogs would you give me half of them?" "That isn't fair!" came the reply. "You know I *have* two hogs!" The man was generous with what he did not have, but was miserly with what he did have.

God's Big Shovel

A man who grew richer even though he gave generously to worthy causes was asked how that was possible. He replied, "I do not know. I just keep shoveling it out, and God keeps shoveling it in. I guess His shovel is bigger than mine."

He Made the Sacrifice

Members of the Dauphin Way Baptist Church, Mobile, Alabama, were asked to give sacrificially to support construction of a new building. One stalwart member had been planning to retire. He realized, however, that if he did so, he would be unable to pledge the amount he wished to give. So he was postponed retirement for three years until his pledge was paid.

GOD'S KINGDOM
CHRIST'S KINGDOM

Building the Kingdom

During World War II someone told a soldier he was building a better world. He replied: "No, I am destroying an evil world. Someone else must build a better one." The kingdom of God is built by men of peace.

His Work, Not Ours

We often speak of *establishing* God's kingdom. However, that is His business, not ours. We are to be witnesses concerning the kingdom and how one can become a part of it.

The Eternal Kingdom of Christ

The once mighty Napoleon is reported to have made this statement: "Alexander, Caesar, Charlemagne, and myself founded empires; but on what foundation did we rest the creatures of our genius? Upon force. But Jesus Christ founded an empire upon love; and at this hour, millions of persons would die for Him.

"I die before my time, and my body will be given back to the earth to become food for the worms. Such is the fate of him who has been called the 'great Napoleon.' What an abyss between my deep misery and the eternal kingdom of Christ, which is proclaimed, loved, adored and is still existing over the whole earth."

GOD'S LOVE

I know not where His islands lift
Their fronded palms in air;
I only know I cannot drift
Beyond His love and care.

—John Greenleaf Whittier
"The Eternal Goodness"

God does not say, "Be good, and I will love you." Rather He says, "Because I love you, you should be good."

God loves humankind not because of what it is but in spite of what it is.

Love's Quiet Confidence

Though waves and storms go o'er my head,
Though strength and health and friends are gone,
Though joys be withered all and dead,
Though every comfort be withdrawn,
On this my steadfast soul relies—
Father, Thy mercy never dies!
Fixed on this ground will I remain,
Though my heart fail and flesh decay:
This anchor shall my soul sustain,
When earth's foundations melt away:
Mercy's full power I then shall prove,
Loved with an everlasting love.

—John Wesley

More Than Enough

A young woman grew up in dire poverty in the heartland of the country. A benefactor made it possible for her to take a trip to the coast where for the first time she saw the ocean. Enraptured she stood gazing at its vastness. In awe she was heard to say, "Thank God for something of which there is more than enough!"

So it is with God's love. We stand in awe of its vastness. There is more than enough!

Unending Love

George Matheson was engaged to be married when he went blind. Rather than face life married to a blind person, the young lady called off the engagement. Brokenhearted, Matheson found solace only in God. Out of this tragic experience he penned the words for a beautiful hymn.

> O love that will not let me go
> I rest my weary soul in thee;
> I give thee back the life I owe,
> That in thine ocean depths its flow
> May richer, fuller be.

Infinite Love

In 1973 a California newspaper carried a story about a discovery made by astronomers in the giant observatory of the University of California. The scientists picked up radio signals from a body in space that they estimated to be fifty million light years from the earth. Prior to that the most distant object known was ten million light years from earth. Distances such as those are beyond our comprehension, but illustrate well the infinite boundaries of God's steadfast love. "For as the heaven is high above the earth, so great is his mercy (steadfast love) toward them that fear him" (Ps. 103:11).

GOD'S OMNISCIENCE

Spiritual leaders come and go, but God and His power are constant.

When you are in a sense of total helplessness, cast yourself into the arms of omnipotence.

We Know So Little

Many people want to limit God's knowledge by theirs. But when we have amassed the total of human understanding, it is like lifting water from the limitless ocean of God's omniscience and wisdom.

He Knows What He's Doing

God has placed every part of the body so that it may function properly. Just suppose that He had placed the nose upside down. You could drown in a rainstorm. Aren't you glad God knows down to the smallest detail what He's doing?

Why Green Pastures?

Has it ever occurred to you why God made grass and tree leaves green? Some years ago our church added a building that included a new office suite. The interior decorator wanted a soft green color scheme in my office. I wanted brighter colors. Finally, she explained to me that because I would spend much time counseling people, most of whom would be in a disturbed emotional state, the green color scheme would be more appropriate. Green soothes the emotions; red excites them. Thus, she had her way.

Shortly after entering the new office, a lady came to see me who was emotionally distraught. After I had counseled and prayed with her, her emotions were more under control. She remarked,

"The green in this office is so soothing!"

So God leads us to lie down in green pastures (Ps. 23:2) to refresh our troubled spirits. Once again, God knew what He was doing.

GOD'S POWER

Someone said that an eagle that soars high above the earth does not worry about how it will cross a river. Our faith in God's power is our eagle's wings.

> Though earth and man were gone
> And suns and universes ceased to be,
> And Thou wert left alone,
> Every existence would exist in Thee.

—Emily Bronte

Whoever considers the study of anatomy, I believe will never be an atheist; the frame of man's body, and the coherence of his parts, being so strange and paradoxical, that I hold it to be the greatest miracle of nature.

—Edward Herbert, Lord of Cherbury

We never really prove the power of God until we attempt the impossible.

Martin Luther's great hymn of the Reformation points us to strength in God and warns us:

> Did we in our own strength confide,
> Our striving would be losing.

The *Cause*

A university physics professor testified that he came to the university believing he had all the answers. "An avowed evolutionist, I knew all about *cause* and *effect*. I could begin with the present and work back. Behind every natural effect I found a natural cause.

"One day I was studying a specimen under a microscope. Sud-

118

denly I noticed a particle of dust on the lens. I asked whence came that dust. That dust was an effect for which I could find no natural cause. I had to admit that behind the dust was not a cause but the *Cause*. A speck of dust led me to God!"

Glory Above the Heavens

The knowledge of modern astronomy exceeds the grasp of the mind of humanity. On March 2, 1982, the news media announced that a satellite launched two years earlier had explored Jupiter and was headed toward the outer reaches of our solar system. Ten years will be required before the satellite arrives there! Still, beyond that will lie what one astronomer has estimated to be fourteen quadrillion solar systems. Each one, like ours, has its own sun and billions of stars. Truly, God has displayed His glory above the heavens (see Ps. 8:3).

Inconceivable Power

Many years ago I spoke at a dinner at a Strategic Air Command (SAC) Base in western Oklahoma. During a tour of the base the commanding officer showed me five large bombers loaded with nuclear weapons. He said that even if someone pushed a button in Omaha, Nebraska in the middle of the night, a signal would sound on this base and these bombers would be in the air in fourteen minutes. I commented that I was sure the United States could protect itself. The commander replied, "Well, that is classified information, but I can tell you in terms of World War II explosives, a train five thousand miles long with each freight car holding one hundred thousand pounds of bombs would be required to carry the load." I asked him to tell me no more, for I could not stand it. So much power for destruction!

Yet the explosives on all those five planes were as firecrackers when compared with the infinite power of God. All His power is for benevolent use and is available to God's people if only they will claim and use it.

Plans to Fit the Power

One of the noblest souls in our denomination is its former president Dr. Carl Bates. He had a dramatic conversion experience in a New Orleans hotel room after reading a Gideon Bible. He says that after being called into the ministry he began to pray for God to give him His power. But he did not receive it. Finally, after many such prayers God gave Him His answer. "With plans no larger than yours, you do not need my power."

GOD'S PRESENCE

As sure as God puts his children in the furnace, he will be in the furnace with them.
—Charles Haddon Spurgeon

Truth forever on the scaffold.
Wrong forever on the throne—
Yet that scaffold sways the future,
And, behind the dim unknown,
Standeth God within the shadow,
Keeping watch above his own.

—James Russell Lowell, "The Present Crisis"

He Keeps the Ship on Course

A ship was caught in the teeth of a storm at sea. The passengers were terrified, thinking that there was no hope for survival. Then one of the passengers went up on the bridge. He regained his peace and calm, for he saw the captain. His face was beaten by the wind and rain, but his hands firmly held the helm. Holding the ship on its course, he had a smile on his face.

So may God's people maintain their peace. God is in control, the master of wind and wave. And *there is a smile on His face*!

A Promise of His Presence

My mother died in 1946. At that time, I had been a pastor for over seventeen years. Hundreds of times I had tried to minister to bereaved families, reading to them the precious promises of God. I believed every one of them, but, since I had not personally experienced the "valley of the shadow of death," I could not enter fully into the sorrow of others or into the comfort of God's Word.

121

As we sat at my mother's funeral, my heart ached. Then Dr. John H. Buchanan, my mother's pastor and my longtime friend, read Isaiah 43:2-3a. I had believed this great promise, but it had never before spoken to me personally. It seemed I was hearing the words for the first time. Through them, God spoke to my need. Suddenly, over me came a calm I cannot describe. It has never left me. The Holy Spirit had made those words my own!

God Has Not Moved

A married couple of many years rode along in their automobile. The wife sat at one end of the seat and the husband at the other end behind the steering wheel. The wife asked, "Why can't we sit close together like we did shortly after our marriage?" Her husband replied, "I ain't moved."

Is your sense of fellowship with God less than it once was? Well, you can be certain of one thing. God hasn't moved, so draw nearer to Him.

He Was There All the Time

The son of an Indian chief had reached the age when he had to prove he was a man. Part of the testing required him to spend a night alone in a forest inhabited by wild animals. All through the night the wild animals gathered around the boy, growling and snarling. If he ran away, he would fail the test. Even though he was frightened, he was determined to stay.

Finally the dawn began to break, and the night shadows began to disappear. The animals slunk away. As the boy began looking around in the morning light, much to his surprise he saw his father stationed behind him with an arrow fixed in his bow. Unknown to the boy, his father had been there all the time to protect his son from harm.

Gods That Are "No-gods"

In Kyoto, Japan, I visited the "Temple of a Thousand and One Gods." The images of the goddess worshiped there had many

arms, depicting her helpfulness. A thousand was considered a perfect number. The reference to a thousand and one denoted infinity.
As I watched, a well-dressed man approached one of the altars. He
clapped his hands three times to let the goddess know he had come
to worship her.

In Bangkok, Thailand, Frances and I saw the "Sleeping Buddha." As I looked upon the prone image with its eyes closed as if in
sleep, I thought of the utter emptiness of paganism.

Then in Jaipur, the pink city of India, we were told we could not
enter one of the temples since it was after 9 o'clock in the evening.
The god was asleep.

We rejoice that the Lord God neither sleeps nor slumbers (see
Isa. 5:27). He is infinite, always present, and able to help us to the
uttermost.

My God is Alive!

Some years ago many people were disturbed by the "God is
dead" philosophy. I was tempted to write a book entitled *My God
Is Alive! Too Bad About Yours!* Had I done so, I simply would
have related the many instances where God had removed obsta-
cles from our path as Frances and I sought to do His will.

GOD'S WILL

One of the devil's favorite methods in thwarting God's will is to seek to entice us to attempt to achieve a worthy goal by unworthy methods.

The Lord God Jehovah is revealed in His name but sometimes concealed in His ways.

> To do or not to do; to have or not to have,
> I leave to Thee:
> Thy only will be done in me;
> All my requests are lost in one,
> "Father, Thy will be done!"

> —Charles Wesley

Dr. George W. Truett on God's Will

Dr. Truett died in July, 1944. To me one of his most memorable statements was about the will of God. He said, "To know the will of God is the greatest knowledge; to do the will of God is the greatest achievement." Then he added, "The will of God is not always easy, but it is always right."

I attended his funeral. As I viewed him in his casket, he held an open New Testament in his left hand. The index finger of his right hand pointed to Matthew 6:10: "Thy will be done." It was the motto of his life. We should make it ours.

In His Will the Walls Fall

Frances and I often talked about our experiences as we sought to follow God's will. At times an obstacle would loom up before us. Had we stopped walking, the obstacle would have become a brick wall. Continuing by faith we often found that the obstacle was but an illusion. At other times we found the wall was like tissue paper that fell apart as we approached it in faith. Trust the Lord in the *now*; leave the future in His hands.

Not a Blanket

Do not speak of God's will as though it is a blanket covering everything that happens to us. God's will has many facets. His will is *purposive, permissive,* and *providential.*

History is to be viewed in light of an *occupied cross*, an *empty tomb*, and the *occupied throne*.

Pillars of the Faith

The three giant pillars of the Christian faith are Jesus' virgin birth, atoning death, and bodily resurrection. Take away any one of these and the structure of Christian faith falls. Taken out of the context of all three, any one of them is without meaning. Considered together, they comprise the greatest story ever told.

You Can't Improve On It

In 1956 Billy Graham conducted a crusade in Oklahoma City. One noonday he spoke to a joint meeting of the city's civic clubs. Dr. Graham's message was a simple sermon on salvation by grace through faith in Jesus Christ.

At the end of the meeting some of the men in attendance rushed forward to thank him for his message. One said, "I have been going to church all my life, but that is the first time I have ever heard that! It is the greatest thing I ever heard."

The Good News

The word *gospel* means good news. Of course, if Jesus only died, that is *bad news*. The fact that He died, the sinless for the sinful, and that He rose triumphant over death and the grave is *good news* indeed.

Nothing But Jesus Christ

Paul Fox was a fellow student in the seminary and remained a friend of mine through the years until his death in 1986.

Shortly after we finished seminary, we met at the Southern Baptist Convention. In a brief conversation he said, "Hobbs, don't ever preach anything except Jesus Christ, and Him crucified." I asked, "Paul, what else is there to preach?" Certainly, without Jesus and all He means to us, we have no gospel.

"The Gospel of Giving"

Several years ago I wrote a book entitled *The Gospel of Giving*. That is what Christianity is all about. God *gave* His Son. The Son *gave* His life. We are exhorted to *give* of our means and ourselves to carry the gospel to all people everywhere.

There's Only One Way

The trend today is toward broadmindedness. Many insist that we should ignore our differences in theology and major on points where we agree. Strangely this attitude is confined to religious matters. We want bankers who are narrow-minded to the extent that two plus two equals four, not three. We insist on a pharmacist following exactly the doctor's prescription. This is true narrow-mindedness. We commend it in matters of lesser importance—finances and health. But many condemn it in the supreme matter of soul salvation.

A Modern Philip

A letter came to the Southern Baptist Radio and Television Commission from a man who lived in Mexico City. One Sunday he drove from there southward. His car radio was on and "The Baptist Hour" was being broadcast. Since he was studying English and I was using well-enunciated English, he decided to listen. I was delivering a simple message on the plan of salvation. When the program was finished, the man said that the message was the most glorious news he had ever heard. *And he had heard it for the first time*!

Later that day he was returning to Mexico City and had stopped to buy gasoline. The service station owner introduced him to a young American man bound for Mexico City. He suggested that the man give the young American a ride. Driving along they became better acquainted. The young man was a Baptist from Knoxville, Tennessee, serving as a missionary among some Mexican Indians. Upon learning this the Mexican asked if he ever heard "The Baptist Hour." The missionary said that he listened when he could.

The man told of his experience earlier in the day. He asked the young American, "Could you tell me how to be saved?" He parked his car alongside the highway. Taking his New Testament the young American missionary explained the plan of salvation to the man and led him to receive Jesus as His Savior.

In his letter to the Radio and Television Commission the man wrote, "I want you to pray that I may lead my wife to have the same experience." About two weeks later a second letter arrived saying that she also had been saved. The man made an additional request. "Will you pray that we may be able to lead our children to know Jesus as their Savior?"

The gospel "is the power of God for salvation" (Rom. 1:16, RSV).

GOSSIP/SPEECH
POWER OF WORDS

To malign a person's character falsely is worse than murder.

Power of Words

The power of words may be seen in recalling the impact of speeches made by Adolf Hitler and Winston Churchill. Through words inflamed with hatred and lies, Hitler whipped his nation into a frenzy to become a juggernaut of destruction. On the other hand, Churchill, armed with eloquent, measured words, lifted his nation from the ashes and debris of defeat to go on to victory.

Gossip and Garbage

A gossiper usually knows where to take his *garbage*. Avoid making your ears someone else's *garbage cans*.

Dogs Carry Bones

An old saying is that a dog that brings a bone also carries a bone. Thus the hearer of contentious talk must be careful what is said to the person bearing the tale. You may be certain that the person who brought the "bone" will make haste to carry one back to somebody else.

The Power of Grievous Words

While in college I was pastor of the Berney Points Baptist Church, Birmingham, Alabama. The church was in walking distance of Rickwood Field where the Birmingham Barons played baseball. As a courtesy the owner gave an annual pass to each pastor in the city. During the Depression, Frances and I had little money, but with my pass I could enjoy the afternoon *free*.

Some games were designated "Ladies Day." Many of the ladies

came to talk instead of to watch the game. Then when the crowd yelled, some lady would ask, "What happened?"

One day I sat behind two ladies, one being of the overstuffed variety. When the heavy lady repeated a catty remark she had made to yet another lady, her friends responded, "You shouldn't have said that!" To which the heavy lady retorted, "Well, I don't care! She said I looked like a mattress tied in the middle!"

Out of such remarks friends are lost and enemies gained. How much better it would have been had she given a soft answer rather than a barbed comeback!

What Profanity Says

Profanity is evidence of ignorance. Those using profane language lack the vocabulary to express themselves without resorting to gutter language. No Christian should be guilty of such unbecoming talk.

Words Get Back to You

The boss spoke harshly to one of his employees, making him mad. Arriving home, the employee had a nasty word for his wife. She yelled at the son. The son kicked the dog. In the yard, the dog bit the boss who had come to apologize for his harsh word.

GRACE

Grace is free, but it makes its demands.

> O God, how beautiful the thought,
> How merciful the blest decree,
> That grace can always be found when sought,
> And nought shut out the soul from thee.
>
> —Eliza Cook

A View of Grace

We may see a person as an alcoholic, a bum, and a human wreck destroyed by sin. God sees not only what we are but what we *may become* by His forgiving grace.

Better Than My Best

While I was in seminary Dr. George W. Truett preached on campus for one week. One day his sermon was on grace. I will never forget one statement he made. "I could not trust my hope of heaven on the best second I ever lived!" I thought, "If he has to say that, what about me?" What about all of us!

"An Experience of Grace"

Kyle M. Yates, Sr., was my teacher in the seminary and my friend through the years. At the time of his death he was distinguished professor of religion at Baylor University. He was a scholar *par excellence* with a warm heart. To recognize this happy combination you have only to read his *Preaching from the Psalms.* He called his treatment of Psalm 40 "An Experience of Grace." He wrote:

The opening verses of Psalm 40 have sung their way into the hearts of countless thousands. Every person who has experienced the saving grace of our divine Redeemer finds in this poem the picture of his own salvation. . . . The rich tones of transforming grace mingle with the groans of the helpless sufferer. The love of God glows in the darkness and brings a miraculous lift to one who dares continue his poignantly pitiful cry for deliverance. In the midst of the changing panorama of events the notes of a *new song* burst out from the throat of the redeemed man. Surely our age needs to hear this song and to pause before the Saviour who makes such a miracle possible.

Choose the Grace Road

A man stands at a fork in the road trying to decide which way to go. One road has a sign which says "law." The other has a sign reading "grace." If he chooses to travel the *law* road, he falls away from the *grace* road. It is not a matter of being in grace, and falling out of it. It is a matter of never having been in grace.

One cannot travel both roads. For law and grace negate each other. If it is by works it cannot be by grace or as a gift. If it is by grace, then it cannot be by law. Christ is in the grace road. So if you travel the law road, you are cut off from Him and His saving power. To depend upon legalism in any form or degree for salvation is to turn your back upon Christ.

HEAVEN

There is a land where everlasting suns shed everlasting brightness; where the soul drinks from the living streams of love that roll by God's high throne! Myriads of glorious ones bring their accepted offerings there. Oh! how blest to look from this dark prison to that shrine, to inhale one breath of Paradise divine, and enter into that eternal rest which unites the sons of God.
      —Sir John Bowring

> If God hath made this world so fair
> Where sin and death abound,
> How beautiful beyond compare
> Will paradise be found.

—James Montgomery

Loved Ones in Heaven

People often ask me if they will know their loved ones in heaven. My reply is that they knew them on earth and that stripped of the limitations of the flesh they will have more intelligence in heaven than they had on earth. This does not mean my wife will be my wife in heaven (see Matt. 2:30). As children of God we will have a relationship far richer and sweeter than any we knew on earth.

Welcome Home!

An aged missionary couple returned to the United States after a lifetime serving the Lord in Africa. They thought of it as a glorious homecoming. On the same ship was a famous personality returning from a six-week game hunt. When the ship docked the hunter was greeted by a large crowd and a marching band. With much fanfare the crowd thronged about the game hunter, leaving the missionary couple standing alone.

The husband complained that this was not fair. The parade should have been for them rather than some great game hunter. Even after they settled in a their small hotel room, he continued to complain. Finally, his wife said, "I'm going out for a little while. While I'm gone I want you to talk to the Lord about your attitude."

When she returned, she asked her husband if he had done as she said. He assured her he had. "Then what did the Lord say?" she inquired. Her husband replied, "The Lord said, 'My child, don't fret. You're not *home* yet.' "

HOLY SPIRIT

Unlike other kinds of power, we do not *harness* God's spiritual power: we *yield* to it in faith.

Indwelling and Filling by the Spirit

The New Testament speaks of Christians being both indwelt and filled by the Holy Spirit. There is a difference between the two.

Through its wiring system a building may be indwelt by electricity. It is filled with its power only as it is allowed to work through electrical appliances: light bulbs, motors, and the like.

At the moment of regeneration the Christian is indwelt by the Holy Spirit (see John 14:17). But the individual is filled by the Spirit when he yields his life to the Spirit's direction and power. If you wish to be filled with the Holy spirit, you must yield your body, your total self, to Him that He might work in and through you.

The Holy Spirit and Prayer

Gardner Taylor is one of America's greatest preachers. Many years ago I heard him say that words are vehicles by which to transfer ideas from one mind to another. However, some ideas are so heavy that the words break down in the effort.

What a blessed assurance it is to know that when words break down in our effort to transmit the deepest longings of our hearts, we have the Divine Helper through whom these yearnings find their way to the mind of our Heavenly Father.

According to Romans 8:26-27 the Holy Spirit takes our inarticulate groanings and verbalizes them to the Father. Through the Holy Spirit of God who indwells you, a groan in your soul can be the most eloquent prayer you ever prayed.

The Holy Spirit Bears Our Infirmities

Now just suppose that you are traveling down the road. You come upon a man who struggles with a 500-pound bale of cotton, trying to lift it on his wagon. You say, "Friend, you have a problem, don't you." He replies, "Yes, I do. Early this morning this bale of cotton fell off my wagon. And I have struggled all day trying to reload it. But I can't! It's too large for me to get a hold of it. Even if I could, it is too heavy for me to lift it! Oh, I do have a problem!"

So you say, "Well, I can help you. You get on the other side of the bale of cotton, and I will get on this side. We will stand face to face. Then we will stoop down and take hold of the bale. Together we will lift it onto the wagon."

"Likewise the Spirit also helpeth our infirmities" (Rom. 8:26). He comes to you, and says, "My child, you have a problem, don't you?" You say, "O blessed Holy Spirit, yes, I do have a problem! I've tried to pray about it. But it is so heavy, so deep, that I cannot put it into words. I just can't pray anymore!"

Notice that the Spirit does not tell you to get out of the way and He will do it for you. He involves you in it. Instead, He says, "I can help you. You get on that side of your problem, and I will get on this side of it. We will stand face to face. Then we will stoop down and take hold of your problem. Then together we will lift it up to the throne of grace."

Are You Available?

A church conducted a lay evangelism institute in which emphasis was placed on the leadership of the Holy Spirit. Afterward for several weeks a group of laymen held a weekly luncheon at which they exchanged experiences.

A physician said that since the institute he had noticed how natural it was to talk with his patients about spiritual matters. He had customarily done so, but he had to inject it into the conversation. "Now," he said, "it just comes about naturally. I do not know why the difference. I suppose it is because the Holy Spirit knows that I am available."

Source of All Power

One measure of man's progress through the ages has been his discovery and use of power: muscular power of both humankind and animals, fire, wind, coal, gas and oil, steam, electricity, and nuclear. Yet strangely and unfortunately, comparatively few have recognized and utilized God's spiritual power. He is omnipotent or all-powerful. Indeed, He is the source of all power. Wherever the Holy Spirit is mentioned in the Bible, He is related to power in one form or another, but the greater emphasis is on spiritual power.

The Absolute Necessity

Recently I decided to spend an evening watching television. The "menu" included a drama and a baseball game. Just as the drama was coming to the climax, the screen went blank and the lights in the house went out. The air-conditioning stopped, too-on a day in which the temperature had reached 100 degrees, a record for that date. This happened at 7:40 p.m. and continued until 3:40 a.m.

What happened? Nothing was wrong with the television set, the lighting system, or the cooling system. However, no power was available to enable the organized mechanics to function.

Churches and denominations are like that. Organization is necessary, but it is useless without power. And the *Power* is the Holy Spirit.

The Holy Spirit at Work

Many years ago when I was pastor of a church in Alabama, I was preaching a revival in the church. On Sunday night the service had been on radio. I had preached a simple sermon on the plan of salvation.

On Monday afternoon I was calling on some of the families on the other side of the city. Suddenly the thought crossed my mind,

"Go to the church." I was to meet the guest singer there at four o'clock, so brushing it aside I continued my planned visitation. But the thought continued. "Go to the church." Finally the thought became so persistent, with seemingly no purpose in doing so, I returned to the church building.

The church secretary had the afternoon off so I was there alone. In a few moments I heard someone at the office door. Turning, I saw a young woman. She asked if I was the pastor. When I told her I was, she asked, "Will you tell me how to be saved?"

We sat on the front pew of the auditorium as she unfolded her story. She lived in a boarding house with her husband. For some time she had been having an adulterous affair with her husband's best friend.

After dinner on the previous evening, all the boarders were visiting in the large living room. The radio was on. Hearing a few words of my sermon, she sat down before the radio on a small stool, turned the volume down low, and listened to the service. At the close of the sermon, she was under conviction by the Holy Spirit. She decided to seek me out to find out how to be saved.

In simple language I told her how to receive Christ as her Savior. That night in the revival service she made a public profession of her faith in Christ, and later I baptized her. She became a faithful Christian and an active church member.

Just suppose she had not been listening to the radio. Just suppose that my sermon had not been on the plan of salvation. Or suppose that she had brushed it off. Suppose that I had not gone to the church. Or that she had come and found no one there. But *supposing* is out of the picture. The Holy Spirit guided the events. He led us together for her salvation and God's glory!

The Spiritual Dynamic

The early church had no buildings, but met in homes. It had a minimum of organization, but it was infused with the Holy Spirit's power. It puts us to shame insofar as spiritual results are concerned.

A friend of mine said in a sermon that should the Holy Spirit suddenly be taken out of this world, 95 percent of what we are doing in our churches would continue. At first I was shocked by this statement. As I pondered it, I knew that he spoke truth. With our numbers, wealth, and means of communication, if we surrendered to the Holy Spirit as did Paul, we could move the entire world toward God!

HONESTY

Falsehood may have its hour, but it has no future.
—Francois D. Pressense

Honesty of thought and speech and written word is a jewel, and they who curb prejudice and seek honorably to know and speak the truth are the only builders of a better life.
—John Galsworthy

If someone told a story that did not seem to hold together, Frances's mother would say, "Now you will have to thicken that up just a little bit."

Can there be a more horrible object in existence than an eloquent man not speaking the truth?
—Thomas Carlyle

An Ever-present Help

A little boy was asked by his Sunday School teacher to define a lie. He said, "A lie is an abomination to the Lord, and an ever-present help in time of trouble." Like many in our day, he had his Scriptures as well as his moral values confused.

He Robbed Us

You can steal from another by false dealing in a business transaction. I learned that the hard way.

Shortly after finishing seminary Frances and I decided we needed a better automobile. Unable to afford a new one we agreed to trade for a good used car. At a certain dealership we thought we had found the car. It had a nice coat of paint, good tires, and a speedometer reading of about 10,000 miles. The sales agent told us the car had belonged to a reputable company in the city and had been used only to drive from the downtown offices to the plant on the edge of town. A trial drive satisfied us, so we bought the car.

Foolishly on my part, I waited until after the purchase was complete before I asked a mechanic friend to check the car out for me. His report was appalling. He said the car had been wrecked and showed me where the car's frame had been straightened. Spray paint on the body of the car under the hood was evidence that it had been repainted. Judging by the wear in the front wheel bearings, my friend estimated that the car had been driven at least 50,000 miles—high mileage in those days. The dealer had robbed us. Not by sticking a gun in our faces, but through lies and false dealings.

Well, we were stuck. However, the story does not end there. About one year later I was a pastor in another town. The car was giving us so much trouble we decided to trade it in on a new car. I told the sales agent the truth about the car—to the last detail. Soon thereafter he sold it to another unsuspecting customer. He only told them it had belonged to his pastor.

The buyer drove the car to Florida. A few weeks later he returned. The car barely crept into the dealership. Instead of the front wheels standing straight, they were at an angle. The wheel bearings were gone. He had had many other troubles with the car as well.

The man said to the sales agent, "Didn't you tell me this car had belonged to your pastor? I would like to have his name and address, for I would like to see the Baptist preacher who could so completely wear out a car in such a few miles!"

As least I learned from the experience. Never buy a used car simply by kicking the tires, looking at the paint, reading the speedometer, or listening to the sales pitch.

HOPE

Hope, like the gleaning taper's light
Adorns and cheers our way;
And still, as darker grows the night
Emits a brighter ray.

—Oliver Goldsmith

Cast all your cares on God! That anchor holds.
—Alfred Tennyson

A Verse of Hope

An old man was asked his favorite Bible verse. He replied, "It's the one that says, 'And it came to pass.' " When questioned why, he answered, "When trouble comes, I just say, 'And it came to pass.' "

Live with Hope

If your business fails, do not sit among its ashes and weep. Clear away the debris and start rebuilding for the future. If a loved one dies, of course you will grieve over your loss. But the death of aloved one does not mean your life is over. Your loved one would not want you to do that. So why should you?

The same holds for any untoward experience you have in life. You are still alive, so go on living. Instead of wasting your time wishing about the past, spend your time and energy building for the future. Take hope!

His Only Hope

At the time Frances and I married I was living in a boarding house. One of the boarders was a self-styled infidel. We had some rather hot discussions as to whether or not there was a God. One day he became painfully ill. That night I decided to look in on him to see how he was doing. As I approached his closed door I heard him talking. Thinking he had a visitor I paused outside the door. After a moment I concluded he was talking to himself. Then I caught his words. Over and over he was saying, "Oh, Lord! Oh, Lord!" In his distress he had shed his outward calm and was actually praying to the Lord." He had come to see the source of hope during his time of distress.

What Assurance!

An English woman had two daughters, one of which had died. She was on a ship bound for America for a visit with her other daughter. In a storm at sea it was feared that the ship might sink. All the passengers save this woman were in a state of near panic. When asked why she was so calm, she said: "Well, I have two daughters, one in America and one in heaven. I am on my way to see my daughter. If the ship survives, I will see the one in America. If not, I will see the one in heaven. So either way, I will see my daughter."

A Lesson in a Song

One of the great Gospel songs tells us to "take your burden to the Lord, and leave it there." The trouble with most of us is that we take our burdens to the Lord, lay them before him, and then take them away again. We should *leave them there*!

HUMILITY

"Get me some great task, ye gods, and I will show you my Spirit!"
"No, no," says the good Heaven, "Plod and plough."
—Ralph Waldo Emerson

Humility, that low, sweet root
From which all heavenly virtues shoot.

—Thomas More

Proud Humility?

Humility is a worthy attitude for any disciple of Jesus. Nevertheless, unless properly regarded, humility itself may become a source of pride.

Look Who Turned Out Really to Be Somebody

Two English brothers took different directions in their lives. One went into diplomatic service to make a name for himself. The other answered the call of God to be a missionary to Africa.

Several years later in a British volume of "Who's Who," many columns were devoted to the missionary brother. Under the long list of his accomplishments appeared the name of his diplomat brother, followed by the simple words "Member of Parliament."

One brother lost his life only to find it; the other sought to save his life only to lose it.

HYPOCRISY

There is no worse epithet to apply to a Christian than *hypocrite*.

The Lord Sees

What a person is on Sunday is to govern his/her actions the rest of the week. A Christian on the Lord's Day is to act like one all the other days. Conversely, a person who is a pagan during the week is seen by God as a pagan on Sunday. What a person is speaks so loudly that God cannot hear what the person claims to be.

Out of the Heart

America is a land filled with church buildings. These buildings are no guarantees of God's favor. He does not count buildings but examines hearts. The real issues of life proceed out of the heart.

Who Are Your Trying to Fool?

During the Prohibition Era I recall seeing a California product called a "grape brick." This was dehydrated juice packaged in the shape of a brick. By mixing the brick with water, it became grape juice. Innocent enough? However, on the package were these words: "Warning: If You Add Sugar Fermentation May Take Place." Obviously, the product was deceptive. It was a way to get around the law to tell buyers how to make wine.

The Facts Didn't Matter

Before I went to college I worked with a man who knew more Bible facts than many preachers. Yet he claimed to be an atheist. He studied the Bible only to argue about it and to try to refute it.

God holds such persons responsible for knowledge about which they do nothing.

Too Much P'lackin'

When I was a little child we used to have "play like" games. Only we shortened it to "p'lack." Someone would say, "Let's p'lack so and so." I suppose children still do. Well, let's do a little "p'lacking."

Let's "p'lack" we are city firemen pitching horseshoes outside the fire station. Calls are coming in that fires are braking out all over town. But we say, "We can't come now. We are playing a game of horseshoes." Or let's "p'lack" we are city policemen. Right in the middle of a game of checkers calls pour in that a crime wave is sweeping the city. But we say, "We can't come now. We are playing checkers." Or let's "p'lack" we are doctors on the golf course. Word comes that an epidemic has broken out. People all over the country are sick and dying. But we say, "We can't come now, for we are playing golf."

Silly? Unheard of? Yes! But not nearly so much like "p'lacking" Christians. We hear God's call to reach out to people who are lost in sin and hell-bound. Sadly, many who claim Jesus as Savior say, "We can't go because we are playing our little games at church."

He Buttered Him Up

British Prime Minister Chamberlain flew home to London after a conference with Hitler and his aides and triumphantly announced that he had "achieved peace in our time." But his words soon mocked him as Hitler loosed his dogs of war on Poland. All Chamberlain got in our time was the bloodiest war in history. He believed the butter-slick mouth of the German dictator, but he did not see the war in his heart (Ps. 55:21).

It Looked Good

An English surgeon was talking to a French colleague about a new type of operation. The Englishman said he had never performed it, whereas the other boasted that he had performed it many times. Astounded, the English surgeon asked about the results. Said the Frenchman, "Oh, they all died. But is was a beautiful operation!" The surgeon was more concerned about appearances than about results.

INDIFFERENCE

Lines of least resistance make crooked rivers and crooked men.
—William H. Danforth

Spiritual cowardice is not only weakness but wickedness.
—J. B. Gambrell

Before Christ there is no neutral ground.

If an indifferent Christian could spend just five minutes in hell he/she would come forth as a flaming evangelist seeking the lost.

Some Day It Won't Be Good Enough

A friend of mine has spent his life in evangelism. Many years ago he told me that, having preached in revivals all over the world, he found the most difficult place for evangelism was in a fertile valley of Southern California. People living there had come from such places as Arkansas, Oklahoma, and Texas with all their earthly goods stacked on old, worn-out automobiles. Now they owned productive farms, lived in fine debt-free homes, and enjoyed all the creature comforts they desired. This friend said when he talked to them about heaven many replied, "Heaven? Southern California is good enough for me."

INFLUENCE

It is well for us to think that no grace or blessing is truly ours until
God has blessed someone else with it through us.
        —Phillip Brooks

I gave a beggar from my little store
Of well earned gold,
He spent the shining ore, and came again and yet again
Still cold and hungry as before.
I gave a thought, and through that thought of mine
He found himself, the man, supreme, divine!
Fed, clothed and crowned with blessings manifold
And now he begs no more.

        —Ella Wheeler Wilcox

Someone said, "It is the law of influence that we become like those
whom we habitually admire. Men are mosaics of other men."

I remember some wise old character saying, "Train up a child in
the way he should go—then go that way yourself—and when he is
old he will not depart from it."

What We Do Matters to Others

A dedicated Christian and/or church will inspire others to do
likewise. When I became pastor of the First Baptist Church, Oklahoma City, Baptist state workers told me that what our church did
affected every other church in the state. When promoting some
program, the first question asked was, "What is the First Baptist
Church, Oklahoma City, doing about it?" As Christians and
churches we have a responsibility toward others.

The Powerful Influence of the Elderly

Frances's mother lived with us while we were in college. This was during the Depression of the 1930s. We could not afford to buy lunch at school. When we returned home in the afternoon, she had a hot meal waiting. This was a ministry she could do for us.

She had two daughters who married Baptist preachers. Our church work took us away from home a great deal, especially for night meetings. When Frances's sister gave birth to a son her mother lived with them and helped care for the child. When our son was born, she did the same for us. In fact, she continued to live with us until her death. She was a blessing to all of us. Through the years our son called her "Mama" and his own mother "Mother." Like Abel (Heb. 11:4), "being dead yet [she] speaketh [continues to speak]" through her children and grandchildren.

Learning at the Feet of the Masters

So much can be learned from our wiser elders—if only we will do so. Two such instances stand out in my memory.

During a revival in First Baptist Church, Lubbock, Texas, B. B. McKinney led the music and I was the preacher. Every free moment I sat at his feet as he told me about many of the hymns he had written. Even now as I sing one of those hymns, I relive the week I spent with him. I was able to look into the soul of one of God's giants.

In 1951 I preached a revival at the Druid Hills Baptist Church, Atlanta, Georgia, where Dr. Louie D. Newton was pastor. He was a walking encyclopedia on Southern Baptist history and had been a participant in many of the events about which I had read. For two weeks I sat at his feet as he talked of other giants of our faith and events of our Baptist heritage. My life will ever be richer because I walked with this man who was wise in heart and mind.

Not *with,* but *in* Me

Manuel Scott is a black preacher—one of the greatest. He is small of stature but a giant in his soul. Cultured and consecrated, he can quote the classics as well as the Bible. His sermons are profound, yet simple. He speaks to both the mind and the soul.

Years ago Scott was preaching at a simultaneous revival breakfast in Oklahoma City. Speaking in a low tone, he thanked us for contributing to his ministry. He said something like this:

"The first time my preaching was exposed to my white brethren was when I was asked to preach at one of your revival breakfasts. Your state director of evangelism heard me. The next winter he had me preach at your state evangelism conference. Later he told the other evangelism directors, who in turn invited me to preach for them. Since then I have been doing it all over the country. When I stand up to preach, so many people stand up *in* me!"

Like Father. . .

A small boy sat at the dinner table shoving in food with both hands. His father said, "Son, don't make a pig out of yourself!" When this didn't slow the boy down, the father asked, "Son, do you know what a pig is?" Still shoving in the food, the boy replied, "Yes, sir. It's an old hog's little boy."

The Influence of Trust

While I was still in the pastorate in Oklahoma City, s small group of us from various religious bodies spent a year praying and developing a program whereby we might work together in matters of mutual interest without compromising our doctrinal positions. When we completed our work we issued a press release stating that we had worked out a program. The details were to be announced in detail at a citywide rally at which Billy Graham would be the speaker.

Although they did not know the details, a group of my fellow pastors criticized me for being involved. Their criticism made for a good press story both locally and nationally.

A reporter in another city called a pastor in his town to ask for a statement. The pastor happened to be a good friend of mine. His reply was, "This is the first I have heard about the matter. But if Herschel Hobbs is involved in it, it is all right." This man was such a friend to me. He did not know the program, but he trusted me.

Like Paul and Timothy

Many years ago I received a long distance phone call from a young man who had recently come to be the pastor of one of the largest churches in Oklahoma. Although he is one of the finest pastors and preachers in our state, he had some doubts because he was coming from a relatively small church.

In his call he expressed his lack of experience in a large church, saying, "I am facing problems here that I did not know existed, and I am coming to you for advice as to how to handle them." As an older pastor I saw they were nothing serious, just run-of-the-mill problems. I gave him some suggestion. Then he thanked me, saying, "I will be coming to you often for advice. You must be my 'Paul' and I will be your 'Timothy.'" Soon he found it unnecessary to consult me, but the bond between us has ripened into a rich friendship. When we write we still address and sign the letters as *Paulos* and *Timotheos*.

They Live on in Me

I was blessed with Christian parents. My father died when I was two and a half years old. I was their only son. My mother did double duty in rearing my sisters and me to become Christians. But I will always be in debt to many men who served as *substitute* fathers to me. In the formative and critical years I recall four men especially: Dr. David M. Gardner, my pastor; W. B. Fowlkes, my Sunday School teacher; P. L. Harrop, my B.Y.P.U. (Baptist Young People's Union) leader; and Pete Lester, my scoutmaster. They have long since gone to be with the Lord, but I know that they live on in me.

Whose Life Is Yours?

Often someone who has chosen to live a sinful life says, "It is my life! I can do with it as I wish!" However, such an attitude will not stand up under examination. No one sins in isolation, for it affects everyone the person touches.

This truth is well illustrated in the case of Achan (Josh 7). His sin affected not only himself but his family and nation. The same is true of each of us.

We would all do well to heed the words of Tennyson in his *Ulysses*. "I am a part of all I have met." And others are a part of you——for good or bad.

I Don't Think I Could Have Made It

Since my plane was arriving late at the Dallas/Ft. Worth airport, I had only ten minutes to catch the connecting flight to Oklahoma City. In that brief time I would have quite a long walk to get to the correct concourse. Therefore, as the plane was pulling up to the unloading gate I explained my situation to the stewardess. A young man overheard me.

As soon as the door opened I started walking as fast as I could. The young man who had been on the flight with me walked alongside me, saying over and over again, "Come on! You can make it!" When we came to his gate he said, "I have to stop here. But go on! You can make it!"

I made it! But without his encouragement I would not have done so.

He Had Been Planting the Seeds

A judge lived on his ranch near Dallas. When he died, his funeral was held at the ranch. there were so many flowers that two trucks were needed to transfer them to the cemetery.

As the flowers were being put on the trucks this deacon-judge watched. He stood beside an old man who had worked on the ranch for many years and said to him, "The Judge certainly received a lot of flowers, didn't he." The man replied, "Yes, sir. But you know the Judge has been planting the seeds for these flowers a long time."

What kind of seeds are you planting?

JESUS CHRIST

Did we in our own strength confide,
Our striving would be losing;
Were not the right Man on our side,
The Man of God's own choosing:
Dost ask who that may be?
Christ Jesus, it is He.
                    —Martin Luther

Makes a New Person

Orating from his park "soapbox," a Communist pointed to an ill-clad man and said, "Communism will put a new suit on that man." Someone in the crowd replied, "Christ will put a new man in that suit."

Christ—the Cohesive Force

In Colossians 1:17 Paul spoke of Christ as the cohesive force that holds the entire universe together as a well-ordered whole—a *cosmos* rather than a *chaos*.

The Regulating Power of Christ

Christ keeps our universe running in split-second accuracy. I was the preacher on "The Baptist Hour" when ground was broken for the present building of The Southern Baptist Radio and Television Commission in Fort Worth. As such I was asked to speak. Ground was to be broken, not with shovels, but by setting off dynamite. With his vivid imagination Paul Stevens, then chief executive of the Radio and Television Commisions, devised a dramatic way of exploding the dynamite.

The dynamite was buried at a safe distance from us and connected to a machine in offices of the company that was to set it off.

Paul gave them the exact time he wanted the dynamite to explode. They set the machine in a position so that at that exact second light from a distant star would shine directly into it. This light would generate a spark that would produce an electric current, run through the wire to the dynamite, and set it off.

Paul told me that during my speech, when he pulled my sleeve, I should pause for about three seconds. I did. Then boom! I resumed my message. The star was not a second early, not a second late. All because of the regulating power of Christ.

The lesson for us is this. If Christ can keep this massive time-piece of the universe running with such exact precision, He certainly can do the same for your life—if only you will submit to Him as Lord.

He Speaks to Every Age

Some people say that Jesus has nothing to say to this enlightened age. The truth is that with all its intellect, this age has never come up to Jesus. His character and truth continue to challenge the slow learners of every age.

Death's Lord

Jesus approached the bier of the deceased son of the widow of Nain (Luke 7:12-15). He spoke to the *corpse*. He did so, expecting to be heard and obeyed. You see, this was *death's Lord* speaking. The dead one sat up and began to speak. He who had been a corpse was no longer dead!

A Child's Only Knowledge of Jesus

In Vacation Bible School in our church we sought to reach children who were not involved in church life. A teacher asked one such boy, "Do you know Jesus Christ?" The boy replied, "Is his middle initial 'H'?" The boy had never heard the name of Jesus except in a profane way. How sad!

He Is the Only One

On my pastor's desk is a plaque which reads, "God so loved the world that he did not send a committee." Instead, He gave His only begotten Son to bear our sins, griefs, and sorrows.

Jesus, the Shepherd

Many years ago Dr. and Mrs. Leo Eddleman were missionaries in Palestine. He told me about seeing many flocks mingled at a watering place. When one shepherd was ready to leave he simply walked away, making a certain sound. Immediately, his sheep separated themselves from the others and followed him. His sheep followed him because they knew his voice.

Jesus if the Good Shepherd who "goeth before...and the sheep follow him: for they know his voice" (John 10:4).

JUDGMENT

If God does not punish America for her sins, He should apologize to Sodom and Gomorrah.
                              —Billy Graham

In *Retribution* Henry Wadsworth Longfellow adapted the words of Friedrich von Logau.

Though the mills of God grind slowly,
Yet they grind exceedingly small;
Though with patience he stands waiting,
with exactness grinds he all.

The final judgment will not determine who is saved and who is lost. It will only declare the person's spiritual condition.

The highway of history is cluttered with the debris of once powerful nations that ignored or forgot God.

> The tissues of life to be
> We weave with colors, all our own;
> And in the field of Destiny
> We reap as we have sown.

—Henry Wadsworth Longfellow

Judgment Is Certain

Moderns may think they are getting away with their sins. Though God is patient He does not forever restrain His judgment. His mills may grind slowly, but they grind with exactness. What a person sows, he/she will reap. Just as surely as there is a seedtime, there is a harvest. And the harvest is always greater in quantity than the sowing.

Go to Your Father's House

Evangelist Angel Martinez says that at the judgment, Jesus will say to God's children, "Come with me into your Father's house." To the children of the devil, he will say, "You go along to your father's house, too."

An Accident or Divine Justice?

A man was a prime suspect in a brutal murder, but all the evidence was circumstantial. Therefore the man was never arrested or tried for the crime.

One night the man was traveling on an interstate highway. Apparently he became drowsy and pulled off the pavement for a short nap. As he slept, a truck loaded with logs came along. Just as the truck passed the man's vehicle, the chain holding the logs in place broke. The logs fell on his car and crushed him to death!

Was it an accident? Or was it the principle of divine justice doing what humanity's system of justice could not do? No one can say with certainty, but it is worthy of thought.

But one thing is certain. A person may escape humanity's system of justice, but he or she cannot escape God's justice. "For we shall all stand before the judgment seat of Christ" (Rom. 14:10b). And from His verdict there is no appeal.

Judgment in Preaching

From experience as a pastor I know that it is easier and more delightful to preach about God's love than about judgment. But both are necessary as conditions demand. A physician would not be your friend if he prescribed salve when he knew that saving your life called for radical surgery. The same applies to the preacher.

It Is for Your Own Good

A parent tells a child not to do something that is bad. If the child does what has been forbidden, then punishment comes. Not to inflict the punishment only encourages the child to do something worse. The parent keeps his/her word and metes out the punishment because the child is loved. In the same way, God keeps His word too but always in love.

A Natural Consequence

God does not punish His people arbitrarily. Punishment comes as the natural consequence of sin. When a gracious God withdraws His protective arm from His people, they are left to the terrible harvest of the evil they have sown.

God Settles His Accounts

Two farmers had adjoining farms. One man was a Christian, the other an unbeliever. The Christian farmer faithfully observed the Lord's Day. He and his family always worshiped in the Lord's house. The unbelieving farmer ignored God and tilled his farm seven days a week. At harvest time his farm showed a larger yield than that of his Christian neighbor. When he taunted his neighbor about this, the latter replied, "God does not settle his accounts in October."

But eventually God does settle them.

LIFE/HUMANITY

Mirrors do not make images, they reflect them. If you do not like what you see when you look into a mirror, you don't need to shatter the glass. Rather try to change yourself.

Some people *exist* to a ripe old age; others may be cut off in the bloom of life. Nevertheless, they *live* more in the short span of years than do many who remain on this earth far beyond the proverbial three-score and ten.

Like fruit as it ages, a person may either *mellow* or *rot*.

Man is greater than a world—than systems of worlds; there is more mystery in the union of soul with body than in the creation of a universe.
—Henry Giles

The time of life is short!
To spend that shortness basely were too long.
—Shakespeare, *King Henry IV*, 5.2

To every man there openeth
A Way, and Ways, and a Way;
The High Soul treads the High Way,
The Low Soul gropes the Low,
And in between, on the misty flats,
The rest drifts to and fro;
And every man decideth
The Way his soul shall go.

—John Oxenham

Some people live their lives like a squirrel in a cage. The faster they run

161

the faster they *must* run to just stay even with the situation.

Someone said that age is a matter of mind. If you do not mind, it does not matter.

> My Soul, sit thou a patient looker-on;
> Judge not the play before the play is done.
> Her plot hath many changes, every day,
> Speaks a new scene; the last act crowns the play.

—Francis Quarles

Look with *Upsight*

A person is not to rely on his or her own understanding or *insight*. At best human knowledge is fragmentary. What may seem best to the individual at the moment may not be best in the long haul. *Upsight*, not insight, is to be the governing factor of life. Then the person will have no reason to have regrets when viewing life from *hindsight*.

The Equation for Life

What a person is $^+$ Jesus Christ $^=$ What the person wants to be.

You See What You Seek

Someone said that a vulture soaring through the air does not see the beautiful landscape, brooks, flowers, and green grass. It sees only the dead rabbit under the bush, because that is what it is seeking.

The Harvest of Life

Lord Byron died at the age of thirty-seven. Looking back over a profligate life, he wrote these words:

> The thorns which I have reap'd are of the tree
> I planted;—they have torn me—and I bleed:

I should have known what fruit would spring from such
a seed.

—Childe Harold's Pilgrimage, Canto IV,
Stanza 10

My days are in the yellow leaf;
The flowers and fruits of love are gone;
The worm, the canker, and the grief
Are mine alone!

—On This Day I Complete My Thirty-sixth Year,
Stanza 2

The Road Signs of Life

As we glibly travel over paved, well-marked highways, it is difficult to realize that when I was a boy very few people owned automobiles. Those who did found scarcely any paved roads, had no
road maps, and for the most part no road signs telling how to get
to a desired destination or the distance to it. It was a venture of hit
or miss, punctuated by stops at farmhouses to ask for directions.
Today we have the advantage of well-marked highways. However
we can ignore the signs and drive ourselves to disaster.

Jesus gives us road signs to life. Each of us are to heed them if
we are to arrive at the desired eternal destination.

Living that Endures

I have lived long enough to know how fleeting are our days on
earth. If a person lives to be seventy years old, that is only 840
months! In light of eternity that is hardly long enough to measure-
—just a passing glimpse. How foolish one is to live for that alone!
We should live and labor for that which endures in God's endless
eternity.

One Wrong Turn

Several years ago I was preaching in a revival meeting in Madi-
son, Mississippi, a few miles out of Jackson. I stayed in a motel in

Jackson. Each night I drove back and forth and so became familiar with the road. One night after the service, a group met in a home for some fellowship. When it was over, I started back to the church building from which I knew the way to the motel. Confused by the darkness, I turned one block too soon. Ere long I realized the surroundings were unfamiliar. Many miles farther, I came to a small town. The only visible light turned out to be in the office of a small motel. The night clerk said I was north of Jackson on the road to Memphis, Tennessee. The farther and faster I had driven, the quicker I had gotten further away from my destination. One wrong turn had made all the difference in the world! Life is like that.

How to Stay Young

Some people are old at thirty; others are young at ninety. The latter do not *resign* from life with the passing of the years. Winter may be in the body, but springtime is ever in their hearts.

What better way is there to remain young in heart than to keep in touch with the Lord and stay busy for Him? If you hope to have such a spirit when evening's shadows begin to fall, you need to start it with the sunrise and maintain it through the heat of the day.

Going Nowhere

A man out for a stroll came on another man digging a ditch. When he asked the man why, the digger said, "I dig the ditch to make money to buy food to give me strength to dig the ditch." Beyond that meaningless cycle, what he did had no purpose. He was like a squirrel in a rotating cage, expending energy in a life going nowhere. Granted the ditch may have been useful to some people, but for the digger it was simply a means of subsistence.

A Stark Reminder of the Need for the Commandment

About 7:15 on the morning of August 20, 1986, one of the worst carnages in murder in Oklahoma history took place. It occurred in the workroom of the post office in the city of Edmond, a quiet community on the edge of Oklahoma City, about three miles from my home.

A postal employee had been told that he would be dismissed if his work did not improve. Thus, that morning he went to the post office carry two semi-automatic pistols with extra clips of ammunition. Apparently his intention was to kill every employee of the post office, male and female. He killed the first person in the parking lot outside the building. When he entered the workroom he began shooting everyone in sight. A few who fled were able to escape. When the massacre was over, however, fifteen people were dead. The murderer then committed suicide.

Life is a precious possession—God's gift to man. Life is to be held sacred. The Lord God stressed that in issuing the Sixth Commandment (Ex. 20:13). This tragic event is a stark reminder that the commandment "Thou shalt not kill" still is needed today.

The Problem of Burnout

A deacon lived a very strenuous life in both his business and his church. One Friday night he commented that he had not taken a vacation in twenty-five years. The next afternoon, while mowing his lawn, he had a heart attack and died. His death may have been premature because he never learned to play.

Many Christians are like that. More and more we read about people who burn out. Those who experience burnout become moody, discouraged, and less effective in their work for the Lord.

Think of Living

Recently in a group I commented that I had engagements scheduled for the next two years. A lady responded, "At our age my husband and I do not even buy green bananas anymore!" Well, I may not live to fill all these engagements. Nevertheless, I am not thinking of dying, but of living. My translation to glory is in the Lord's hands. However, I make my plans as though I am going to live a long time. Our life-style should be based on the probability that we will die today. Our life plans should be made as if we would live for many years to come.

The Alternative to Aging

Does someone say, "I don't want to grow old?" Then die young! That is your only alternative. In a certain cosmetics ad on television a beautiful adult forty years of age says, "I am not going to grow old gracefully. I intend to fight it all the way."

Hearing her remark, I thought, *Young lady, you may fight it in your facial appearance. But the vital organs of your body are counting every hour, day, and year.* You may "fool Mother Nature" on the outside but not on the inside. So just plan to grow old gracefully and actively. Such an attitude is indeed one of God's rewards for a life well-used for Him.

Staying Busy

According to Joshua 14:10-12 Caleb did not retire at age 65. Medical science has found that people who have been active all their lives and who suddenly retire with nothing to occupy their time and energy do not live long. A medical doctor told me that when people stop using their minds they become senile and soon die. As for Caleb, the acorn had not been planted from which would grow an oak tree whose wood would be used to make him a rocking chair. In that sense, at least, I share Caleb's spirit. Often I have said that when I die I hope I am so busy for the Lord that I will run a block before I fall!

Learning from Experience

We live in an age when many parents give their children more material things than they can use or appreciate. Children tend to take these things for granted. To describe to the later generations the sufferings of the Great Depression of the 1930s is like describing a sunset to a person born blind or the beauty of a symphony to one born without hearing. The description is not adequate. Experience becomes the best teacher.

Each generation needs to learn from the ones preceding it, building upon the knowledge learned by both the failure and success of former generations. But strangely, where morals are concerned many in every generation want to go back to the Garden of Eden and learn for themselves. Thus we go on making the same old mistakes and sinning the same old sins—with the same tragic results that characterize every age.

What an Education

In a former pastorate of mine we observed "Christian Education Day." One feature was to have each college graduate name his/her Alma Mater along with its colors. One man stood up whom I knew had never attended college. When asked to name his school, he said, "The College of Hard Knocks, colors black and blue!"

LORD'S DAY

"Blue Monday" usually follows "Abused Sunday."

Even Machines Need Rest

Years ago, I read about a railroad that conducted an experiment. It purchased two new locomotives. One was kept in constant service, regardless of Sunday. In the use of the other, late each Saturday they pulled its fire and released the steam. On Sunday it was allowed to cool down, thus re-tempering its metal. Then it was fired up again on Monday. Over the years they found that they had less maintenance and trouble with the latter than with the former. If *rest* one day each week so benefited a piece of machinery, how much more does the fragile, delicate human body and spirit need it!

A Lesson from Atheists

Several years ago some friends and Frances and I spent a weekend in Moscow. We attended Sunday worship services at the Moscow Baptist Church, one of the most Spirit-filled services I ever experienced. Since we were leaving Russian the next day, the wives wanted to shop for some remembrances of the brief visit. Our tour guide was a lovely Russian lady. She said we could window-shop, but we would have to wait until the next day to buy things. When we asked why, she said, "Because it is Sunday and all the stores are closed."

In our so-called Christian nation, Sunday is business as usual. However in a country whose official position is to deny God, all the stores were closed on the Lord's Day.

Singing for a Day of Rest

I grew up in the Deep South. Before the era of mechanized farming large plantations had many black field hands. As they worked, they sang. Sometimes they sang in chorus; at other times only one person sang. One little song went like this. "Come day, go day, God send Sunday." The hard-working field hands looked forward to a day of rest. That was one of God's intentions for the sabbath.

The Best Weather for Sunday

I became pastor of the Dauphin Way Baptist Church, Mobile, Alabama, on January 1, 1945. The first ten Sundays were rainy. Nevertheless we had large attendance at both Sunday School and worship services.

One Sunday in early March I said to the people, "If we had just one pretty weekend, what *could* we do?" Later I learned that one lady had responded, "We'd show him what we could do. We'd go across the bay."

The next Sunday I said, "Finally I have learned how to pray about the weekend weather. I do not pray for rain. The people would stay at home. I do not pray for pretty weather. The people would go across the bay. I pray for threatening weather. That will keep you in town, but will allow you to come to church."

It's His Option

A college ministerial student invited his Bible professor to preach in his church one Sunday. They awoke Sunday morning to find that it was raining. To the young preacher's complaint the wise old professor replied, "Well, it is the Lord's Day and the Lord's weather. If he wants to send them both at the same time, I am not going to complain."

LOVE FOR OTHERS

Some people do good because law *requires* it. Others do good because love *desires* it.

> O Brother Man, fold to thy heart thy brother
> Where pity dwells, the love of God is there;
> To worship rightfully is to love each other,
> Each smile a psalm, each kindly deed a prayer.
>
> —John Greenleaf Whittier

> Oh, how skillful grows the hand
> That obeyeth love's command;
> It is the heart, and not the brain
> That to the highest doth attain.
> And he who follows love's behest
> Far exceedeth all the rest.
>
> —Henry Wadsworth Longfellow

The Greater Circle

In his poem *Outwitted* Edwin Markham wrote:

> He drew a circle that shut me out—
> Heretic, rebel, a thing to flout.
> But Love and I had a wit to win:
> We drew a circle that took him in.

Ministry to Others

Following World War II, C. Oscar Johnson, a Saint Louis pastor, was leading a drive to raise money to feed the war-ravaged people of Europe. Noting the primacy of spiritual ministry he added: "But if we do not feed them now, they will soon not be alive for us to preach the gospel to them." By ministering to men's physical needs, Christians can demonstrate their love and God's love for persons' bodies and souls.

Why Do You Care About Them?

One old comic strip character noted that a stranger came to his church the previous Sunday. No one paid him any mind until the offering plate was passed. The stranger put a large bill in the plate. After church, said the character, everybody "howdydood him to death." Does that sound like James 2:1-7?

Superiority of Christian Love

Christian love rises above human differences to show itself in absolute loyalty to others in their need. Christian love looks on other persons through the eyes and with the heart of God. Christian love respects others as persons who are objects of God's love.

Who Is My Neighbor?

In the parable of the Good Samaritan (Luke 10:30-36) Jesus did not *define* the word *neighbor*. He *described* a neighbor. He was dealing with *actions*, not *academics*.

Love Is Reason Enough

A major television network carried a news story showing a convoy of trucks entering a Thai village. The trucks were loaded with food sent to that village by people in the state of Michigan. The state governor had visited the village and observed the hunger of the people. He returned to Michigan and attempted to do something about it. The people of that little Thai village probably knew little of this place in the United States. Nevertheless, they did know that somewhere there were some people who cared enough to help. Love is reason enough.

Now and Then

In one of his seminary class lectures in New Testament, Dr. A. T. Robertson noted that in heaven all of God's children will love one another. Then he remarked, "Since that is true, we should practice loving each other here on earth."

Justice May Be Blind, But Not Deaf

Joseph Addison wrote, "Justice discards party, friendship, and kindred, and is therefore represented as blind."

It is true that justice is blind, but it is not deaf or mute. Justice hears the cries of the helpless—and the voice of God. Justice cries out against a person's inhumanity to another person.

Henry Drummond on "Love"

Henry Drummond is best known for his little book on love, *The Greatest Thing in the World*. His words on love speak volumes on our hearts: "Instead of allowing yourself to be so unhappy, just let your love grow as God wants it to grow; seek goodness in others, love more persons more; love them more personally, more unselfishly, without thought of return. The return, never fear, will take care of itself."

One in Love

In our country we tend to stress our denominational differences. Frances and I have found that on the mission fields this is not the case. For instance, in Korea we found that, regardless of denominational ties, on Sunday afternoons all the missionaries gathered for a worship service. In an ocean of paganism they were an island of love as they worshiped the Lord who told believers to love one another.

One of the greatest of the early Christians, Florens Tertullian (about A.D. 155-222) said, "See how these Christians love one another." They were simply obeying the command of their Lord. Would that we would do the same!

Warts and All

Years ago my teacher, A. T. Robertson, said to our class, "Young men, when you become the pastor of a church you must love the people—warts and all." Churches have some of all kinds of people. It may be that the "warts" need us most of all.

Sermons in Shoes

In Birmingham, Alabama, many years ago lived a Presbyterian pastor, James Bryan. Throughout the city he was known as "Brother Bryan." There were many preachers stronger in pulpit oratory, but none preached better sermons than he did with his life. Like Jesus, he went about doing good.

It was a common thing for him to come home on a cold day without his overcoat. He had given it to some poor man who had none. One spring day he was driving a horse and buggy through the countryside. He saw a farmer standing dejectedly in the field. It was time for his spring plowing, but his only horse lay dead. Brother Bryan unhitched his horse and gave it to the man, and then walked home.

It was fitting that when his biography was written it was called *A Sermon in Shoes*. John Donne might well have had persons like him in mind when he said, "Of all the commentaries on the Scriptures, good examples are the best." Go, and do thou likewise!

Love Made Him Stay

John Fawcett was pastor of a small Baptist church in an English village. He was called by a much larger church in London. As the movers were loading the household goods on their wagons, the pastor's family and church members wept as they watched. Finally he told the movers to put the furniture back in the house. Said he, "We aren't going!"Out of this experience John Fawcett wrote the following words:

Blest be the tie that binds

Our hearts in Christian love;
The fellowship of kindred minds
Is like to that above.

Before our Father's throne,
We pour our ardent prayers;
Our fears, our hopes, our aims are one,
Our comforts and our cares.

We share our mutual woes,
Our mutual burdens bear;
And often for each other flows
The sympathizing tear.

When we asunder part,
It gives us inward pain;
But we shall still be joined in heart,
And hope to meet again.

Precious Love of a Friend

It was easy for me to love J. D. Grey. He was the kind of friend who was always looking for ways to do nice things for his friends, expecting nothing in return. For instance, though we had never met, when I was called to the Emmanuel Baptist Church, Alexandria, Louisiana, he was the first person to write a letter welcoming me to the state. The first time we met, I knew I had found a kindred spirit.

For years we had an agreement that whichever one died first, the other would conduct his funeral. I conducted his. Our wives also were kindred souls. My wife, Frances, had wanted J. D. to give the eulogy at her funeral. But he was ill and could not come. Less than five months later I gave the eulogy at Lillian Grey's funeral. Five months later I delivered J. D.'s eulogy.

During his terminal illness I called him regularly. He talked with me from his hospital bed. Each time his voice was weaker.

Even when it got so weak I could not understand him, I never let him know it. I just let him talk. The last words he uttered that I understood were "I love you." Precious words! Precious memories!

MARRIAGE

How to Love Your Wife

In jest I used to say, "I love all my wife's relatives, but I love her husband most of all." In my judgment this catches the meaning of Paul's words in Ephesians 5:28-29. The home has no need for a *boss*. In Christian love the husband and wife work together, each in his/her own way, living and loving, laughing and weeping, planning and working toward the common goal of maintaining a Christian home and family.

A Model Marriage

Until the Lord called her home, for over fifty-seven years Frances and I had as nearly perfect a marriage as one could imagine. During her terminal illness she talked about her view of her role as my wife. She always considered her role as being to do what she could to enable me to pursue God's call. She expressed to our children and her sister that she had only one concern about her illness. She did not want to be a hindrance to my work—she felt I should be out preaching the gospel instead of having to look after her. Hearing of it, I told her she was no hindrance. Instead she had been my inspiration and strength through the years. I assured her the same Bible that said to preach the gospel also said that a man who did not look after his household was worse than a heathen. Precious, precious memories! I could wish for every couple a marriage such as ours!

Love that Grows

When Frances and I married, I thought I loved her then all that it was possible to do so. But after more than fifty-seven years, when she went to be with the Lord, I loved her so much more that words could not express it.

A Simple Beginning

Frances and I gave a Valentine's Day party for the deacons and their wives. One game we played called for the husband to describe his wife the first time he saw her. The wife was to tell how her husband proposed and how she accepted. Some of the stories were quite romantic, but one involved a husband who never used two words when one would do. His wife's account of his proposal was: "Oh, he just asked, 'What about it?' and I said, 'Okay!' " With that simple exchange, Bernard and Annie Mae began a genuine, long, happy marriage.

Cooperation, Not Coercion

Cooperation between husband and wife is the norm in the Christian home. When I felt led of God to leave Mobile for Oklahoma City, our son did not want to leave his friends. He asked, "Mother, do we have to go?" She said, "Well, Daddy feels God leading him, and we will go where he goes." I did not *demand* it. She gave it with her whole heart.

It's Only the Beginning

Through the years in wedding rehearsals I have gone through the marriage ceremony with the couple. I end by saying, "When I say, 'I pronounce you wedded, husband and wife,' I have *finished* and you have *started*."

A 50/50 Proposition

Through the years I have counseled may young couples facing marriage. I have told them that personal relationships are a 50/50 proposition. Some days it may be more like 100/0. Other days it may be more like 0/100. But it all balances out to 50/50. To be sure, couples are to avoid problems that harm their relationship. However, try as they may, problems will come. When they do, *giving* and *forgiving* are necessary to maintain the relationship.

One Flesh, But Not One Mind

One man said that in thirty-five years of marriage he and his wife had never spoken a cross word to each other. In his case I suspect that one of three things was true. Either he was not telling the truth, he had a bad memory, or he was so hen-pecked that he dared not open his mouth around his wife.

When two people marry, they become one flesh but not one mind. They will have their differences of opinion, but these are swallowed up in their love for each another.

She Knew the Real Truth

A husband was boasting to some friends about his accomplishments. All the while his wife smiled in silence, knowing who had made him who he was. She would have done well to puncture his balloon of pride and let him see himself as others saw him.

Some Assembly Required

We often say that marriages are made in heaven. The fact is that the institution of marriage was made in heaven. In each individual marriage, however, God gives the couple a "Do It Yourself Kit." They are to work out the marriage on earth. This "kit" consists of the teachings of the Bible concerning marriage.

MATERIALISM/MONEY

An old Roman proverb says that money is like sea water. The more you drink the thirstier you get.

We go into debt to keep up with the Joneses who have already gone into debt to stay ahead of us.

A Spanish proverb says, "There are no pockets in a shroud."

A schoolboy identified what parts of speech *my* and *mine* were. He said they were "aggressive pronouns."

Two thin dimes placed over your eyes can shut out the beautiful vistas of nature.

The Tyranny of Undedicated Wealth

A happy couple won a multimillion dollar lottery. At the time the man had a job that paid $245 per week. When asked what he was going to do with the money, he said, "I am going to take a long vacation and rest." After that he had no plans.

Whether or not this money proves to be a blessing or a curse depends on his attitude toward it and what he does with it.

An anonymous poet warns us at this point.

> Dug from the mountainside, washed in the glen,
> Servant am I, or the master of men;
> Steal me, I curse you,
> Earn me, I bless you,
> Grasp me and hoard me, a fiend shall possess you;
> Lie for me, die for me, covet me, take me,
> Angel or devil, I am what you make me.

A Study in Values

A few years ago some men sought to get a corner on the silver market. This resulted in a sharp upswing in the price of silver. So much so that silverware became a prime target for thieves.

In addition to our regular family silverware, we had quite an accumulation of sterling silver items given to us by churches over the years. For insurance purposes Frances had made an inventory of these. Due to the increase in the price of silver, she decided we should upgrade our insurance. Using a catalog furnished by our jeweler, she was amazed at the increased value of our silver possessions.

But eventually the tide turned. The glut of the market so decreased the value of silver that those who tried to corner the market lost a fabulous sum of money. The drop in price was such that, considering inflation, the value of our silverware returned to what it was before the upswing.

This is just one example of the uncertainty of material values. One who rests his hope on such is building on sand, even quicksand.

The real and abiding values in life are spiritual: God in His three-fold revelation, His Word, redemption, soul security, love, truth, purity—to name a few. It is no wonder that Jesus closed the Sermon on the Mount with the parable of the two builders. Which kind of builder are you?

Greed Is Not Fair

A "Gasoline Alley" comic strip pictured an unscrupulous man doing a mail-order business selling money bracelets. His sales pitch was that if you wore one of the bracelets, money would come to you. With money piled on his desk, the man said, "Well, at least, it comes to me.

No Better Way

A man did a great favor for another man. The recipient of the favor said, "I wish I knew some way to show my appreciation." The other replied. "Since the Phoenicians invented money, they have not improved on that."

Let Me Share the "Bother"

A very wealthy man said, "I can wear only one suit at a time, eat one meal at a time, and sleep in only one bed at a time. Beyond that all my money is a bother." Of course, many would be willing to share his "bother." What he meant was that there is a limit to what material things can do for a person.

Money Can't Buy Everything

Money has power. But it also has weaknesses. For instance, money can buy *land*, but not *love*; *bonds*, but not *brotherhood*; *gold*, but not *gladness*; *silver*, but not *sincerity*; *hospitals*, but not *health*; *condominiums*, but not *character*; *houses*, but not *homes*; *timber*, but not *truth*. Money can purchase *commodities*, but not *comfort*; *ranches*, but not *righteousness*; *ships*, but not *salvation*; and *hotels*, but not *heaven*. To *save* your money you must *share* it; to *love* it is to *lose* it; and to *invest* it forever, you must put it in things *eternal*.

You Can Be Sure He Does

A widow who owned large tracts of oil-rich land was wooed by a fortune hunter. He said to her, "I love the very ground on which you stand."

MIRACLES

Two Miracles

Dr. T. L. Holcomb preached a revival for me many years ago. His message was on the feeding of the multitude as recorded in John 6:5-13. Dr. Holcomb noted that two miracles took place that day. One was that Jesus fed the crowd with the boy's small lunch. The other miracle was that at three o'clock in the afternoon that the boy still had his lunch in the first place!

Miracles Are Easy to Accept

If you accept the first four words in the Bible—"In the beginning God"—believing miracles comes easily. A miracle is an act of God. It is an act contrary to natural law as we understand it, but not contrary to natural law as God understands it. Miracles are actions He performs for the furtherance of His benevolent and redemptive purpose.

God and Miracles

It is quite clear God performed a miracle at Jordan. Many times I have been asked, "Why does not God work such miracles today?" The question is not whether He can, but how He chooses to work. God reveals Himself in terms of people's spiritual development and ability to receive and comprehend the revelation.

God Can *Really* Do It

Many years ago Cecil B. DeMille made his epic film "The Ten Commandments." To create the effect of parting the water he used a large quantity of gelatin. A large fan blew into it, producing the phenomenon of divided water. Then through some photographic method he showed the people passing through it. If the genius of a man could devise such, who can deny to God the power to do the real thing?

Modern-day Miracles

Many professing Christians claim that miracles died out with the apostolic era. Yet, these believers claim that people are still being saved today. If there are no miracles, there is a tragic contradiction here. No miracles? Then no one is being converted--because when a person is born again through the agency of the Holy Spirit, that is one of God's greatest miracles.

MISSIONS

The world's great heart is aching,
Aching fiercely in the night;
And God alone can heal it,
And God alone give light;
And the ones to take that message
To bear the living Word
Are you and I, my Brother,
And the millions who have heard.

—Anonymous

What Is Missions?

R. Keith Parks offers this excellent definition or description of missions (*World in View*, [Birmingham: New Hope, 1987], p.16): "Missions is God's redemption proclaimed through persons to all people. The source is God. Its embodiment is Jesus Christ. Its story is the Bible. Its purpose is salvation. Its scope is humanity. Its declaration is the believer's mandate. Its fulfillment is the church's task. Its application is the world's hope. Its culmination is God's glory."

You Almost Waited too Long

Roger Shelton, a pastor from Nashville, Tennessee, was in Pusan, Korea, on an evangelistic mission. With an interpreter, he visited a man who had creeping paralysis. Both of his legs were paralyzed and the disease threatened his life if no cure could be found.

Entering a dimly lighted room, Shelton found the man crouched on the floor. Speaking through the interpreter, he told the stricken man he had come to talk with him about Jesus Christ. The Korean replied, "I know. I have been waiting for you a long time." The interpreter responded by saying they had arrived at the appointed time.

The Korean explained. "That's not what I meant. My people are Buddhist, and I have been a Buddhist. But Buddha gives me no comfort." Then he pointed to a Korean Bible. He noted that he had read through it twice. "It tells of a great one. I have waited for someone to come and tell me more about him." He said that he had believed that if the Bible was true, God would send someone to tell him.

Shelton told the man about Jesus. He readily believed. As they were leaving, the man thanked them for coming. Shelton said, however, that the man's final words shook every fiber of his emotional being.

"You almost waited too long."

Missions in the Bible

The teacher of a men's class in a Baptist church in a North Alabama city was invited to teach the men's class in a nearby country church. He knew the regular teacher of this class was strongly anti-missionary. It happened that the lesson for that Sunday was on foreign missions. The visiting teacher did not want to offend the regular teacher or get into an argument with him during the lesson.

To avoid both the guest began in Genesis and went through the Bible making a list of missionary verses. Before teaching, he asked the regular teacher to read the verses without comment.

After reading several of the verses, he stopped. Then he spoke to the class. "I just declar' before goodness, the fudder you go the worser it gits!"

This will be the experience of anyone who tries to make a case against missions from the Bible.

The "Ground" of Missions

Dr. George W. Truett was fond of quoting Psalm 24:1 in support of missions. He would say that the church that is not missionary does not deserve the ground upon which its building stand.

Players or Soldiers?

The apostle Paul was committed to preaching the gospel. In Acts 21:10 he expressed the depth of that commitment by saying he was willing to die if necessary.

What a wonderful thing it would be if all Christians had this commitment to duty! Whereas we are now *playing* at the game of missions, the churches would truly be bands of "Christian soldiers, marching as to war."

Missions Makes a Difference

Two Americans were dinner guests of a tribal chief in a South Pacific island. The subject of missions came up. One of the Americans said he didn't believe in missions. The host expressed surprise. Then he remarked: "You should believe in missions. Until a few years ago I was a cannibal, but a missionary came to my island and won me to Christ. Otherwise, instead of you being my dinner guest, you would be my dinner."

Missions to the Heathen

A church was receiving a special offering for missions. One man even refused to pass the offering plate to the next person in the pew. Angrily he said, "I don't believe in missions." Gently the usher whispered to him, "Then I suggest you take some out of the plate. It *is* for the heathen, you know."

Adapting to Existing Circumstances

Dr. Wayne Dehoney's *The Dragon and the Lamb* is the story of the resurrected churches in China. In a simple yet profound style, the book intermingles ancient and modern Chinese history with the Christian movement in this most populous nation on earth.

With the Communist takeover, Christian missionaries were barred from China. Christianity largely went underground in the form of "house churches." A few years ago the Chinese govern-

ment implemented more of an open-door policy toward the outside world. Companion to this was more tolerance toward religion, including Christianity. Church buildings, once confiscated
for other purposes, were returned to the churches. Public worship
was permitted; and despite long years of persecution, Christianity
was found to be "alive and well" in China.

Nevertheless, the Chinese government remained wary of foreign missionaries. While Dr. Dehoney did not see a door opening
for missionaries in the foreseeable future, he added, "The door to
individual Christian involvement is not closed. China gladly wel-
comes individuals who have a skill or technical training that China needs and are willing to come and help the Chinese people." He
mentioned "agricultural experts, public health and social workers,
teachers (especially English), business experts, doctors, etc."

For example, in 1987 Mrs. Baker James Cauthen taught
English at a Chinese university. Born in China of missionary parents, she was a former missionary in China and wife of the late,
longtime president of the Southern Baptist Foreign Mission
Board. However, she served not under the auspices of a mission
board, but as an individual on mission.

To bear witness for Christ calls for individuals who are willing
to adapt to existing circumstances and go on mission for Him.

Finishing What He Began

Many years ago I preached a revival meeting in Taejon, Korea.
A new missionary family had recently come to Korea and was
doing language study in Taejon. Prior to his appointment, the missionary husband had been pastor of a Baptist church near the Air
Force base at Biloxi, Mississippi. While pastor he had invited to
his church a young Korean flyer who was in training at Biloxi. For
some time the pastor preached to the flyer and witnessed to him
about Christ. The flyer returned to Korea, however, without making a profession of faith.

After the missionary arrived in Taejon, he met this former flyer,
now a civilian, walking along the streets of the city. He invited the

man to attend the revival service that night. He did and was saved! When the missionary told me the whole story, I said, "You had to come to Taejon to finish what you began in Biloxi." The story also reminds us that "foreign missions" can be found all about us.

Missions Means Growth

In 1814 the Baptists of the United States were divided almost equally over the matter of foreign missions. Adoniram and Ann Hasseltine Judson and Luther Rice, a bachelor, had been appointed by the Congregationalists as missionaries to India. Rice and the Judsons journeyed to India on different ships. While en route the three studied the issue of baptism. By the time they arrived in India they found they agreed on this issue with the Baptists. Therefore, the three missionaries were immersed by the Baptist missionaries already in India.

Obviously Rice and the Judsons could no longer expect financial support from the Congregationalists. So Rice returned to America to enlist Baptist support for their work. His challenge resulted in a division among the Baptists into missionary and non-missionary groups.

Today the non-missionary group has dwindled into a relatively small entity. Missionary Baptists have grown into the largest evangelical, religious body in the nation. This is especially true of Southern Baptists.

"The Multiple Meaning of Missions"

In my first book, *Cowards or Conquerors*, I included a chapter on "The Multiple Meaning of Missions." My four sub-points were "Missions, the Heartbeat of God;" "Missions, the Theme of the Bible;" "Missions, the Lifeblood of the Church;" and "Missions, the Hope of the World."

A Place of Honor

In Westminster Abbey in London many of the British Empire's greats are buried; such as kings, a queen, statesmen, generals, men of literature, and the like. To my delightful surprise, in one of my visits there I learned that the most honored spot, in front of the altar, is the burial place of a missionary—David Livingstone. This place of honor is a fitting tribute, not only to him, but to people through the centuries who have answered God's missionary call.

A Missionary's Hands

In 1962 Frances and I made a mission tour of Latin America, West Africa, and Western Europe. One stop was at Nelerigu, Ghana. Southern Baptists had a hospital and church there. Both were presided over by Dr. George Faile, a medical missionary from South Carolina. He met us at the airport. On the long drive to Nelerigu, he had to change a tire on the lorry. When we arrived at the mission compound he found that the pump that supplied water to the guest houses was not working. So he fixed it too.

The next morning a large crowd of outpatients was waiting at the hospital. One man had walked thirty-five miles to get there! After a brief evangelistic service, which I conducted, the patients lined up. As they went by, Dr. Faile examined each one. He also filled a prescription of medicine for each person. That afternoon Dr. Faile visited each inpatient at the hospital. Later, as Frances and I watched, he performed surgery on a woman's eyelids.

Before going to bed that night, Frances and I recalled the events of the past twenty-four hours. We had seen Dr. Faile use his hands to change a tire, fix a water pump, examine outpatients, fill prescriptions, tend to hospital inpatients, and perform a delicate operation. To this day, I have never forgotten that dedicated missionary's hands.

All on Mission

Many years ago in seminary chapel Dr. W. O. Carver, professor of missions, introduced the speaker Dr. Everett Gill, Sr. He had just retired after thirty-five years as a missionary in Europe. Noting that Dr. Carver called him a *foreign missionary*, he replied, "The only *foreign* missionary was Jesus Christ who was sent from heaven to earth. I am simply a *missionary* in Europe, even as you young men are missionaries wherever you serve in the United States."

How Long Must They Wait?

Jesus lived and wrought at a strategic time in history. Paganism had proved to be empty vagaries. Pagans turned to their political leaders for salvation, only to find none. The Roman world was overrun with all kinds of religious sects promising spiritual deliverance, but providing none. Many pagans turned to Judaism, only to find it to be rote ritual, ceremonies, and burdensome legalism.

The fog of despair settled over the world. Confusion reigned. Hope was gone. "When the fullness of the time [a time right in God's eyes] was come, God sent forth his Son, made of a woman, made under the law, To redeem them that were under the law, that we might receive the adoption of sons" (Gal. 4:4-5).

Darkness and confusion still reign over the earth. Billions have never heard the gospel of the atoning, living, reigning, and coming Christ. The cry still is heard, "How long must we wait?"

To us He has entrusted the gospel. How long must the masses of the world wait to hear it? The answer lies with you and me.

NEW BIRTH
NEW LIFE

The Way to Spiritual Relationships

A natural birth ushers a person into natural, human relationships. To be ushered into spiritual relationships calls for a spiritual birth—a birth from above.

One and the Same

A strange phrase that has crept into our vocabulary in recent years is "born-again Christian." The phrase is redundant. It is like saying "dog dog." The phrase suggests there is more than one kind of Christian. There is not! If you are born again, you are a Christian. If you are a Christian in the scriptural sense, you have been born again!

Beyond Explanation

A physician said to a pastor, "If you will explain to me the spiritual birth, I will become a Christian." The pastor replied, "If you will explain the natural birth to me, then I will explain the spiritual birth to you." Neither is possible. In both cases we can observe and cooperate with certain processes, but we cannot explain the why, apart from the power of God.

OBEDIENCE

A person must first learn to obey before being qualified to lead.

The Ease of Obedience

William Paley once said, "One very common error misleads the opinion of mankind—that authority is pleasant and submission painful. In the general course of human affairs the very reverse of this is nearer the truth. Command is anxiety; obedience is ease."

If this is true at the human level, how much more is it the case in the divine-human relationship.

Good Flows from Obedience

George Eliot asks and answers a question. "How will you find good? It is not a thing of choices; it is a river that flows from the foot of the invisible throne, and flows by the path of obedience."

PEACE

Shakespeare spoke for all normal people when he wrote: " 'Tis death to me to be at enmity; I hate it, and desire all men's love."

> Peace hath her victories
> no less renown'd than war.
> —John Milton

Whence Come Wars

In 1930 a movie was made about World War I called "All Quiet on the Western Front." In one scene some American "doughboys" were talking. A comic character asked, "Where do wars come from anyway?" Another replied, "Well, one country gets mad at another country, and they start fighting." The first soldier asked, "Do you mean that one piece of land gets mad at another piece of land?" "No," the other replied. "The people of one country get mad at the people of the other." The first soldier picked up his rifle and started walking away. When asked where he was going, he said, "I'm going home. I'm not mad at anybody."

Way to Lasting Peace

The United Nations has not brought an end to war. However, who can say whether we would have had many more wars without it? At least it provides a forum for discussion of conflicting ideologies. Much of its ineffectiveness is because many involved nations either deny God exists or else worship deities other than God. The United Nations makes one thing quite clear. Lasting peace will come, not through human diplomacy, but through submission to

God who has revealed Himself through our Lord Jesus Christ.

Winning the War but Losing the Peace

At the end of World War I, Woodrow Wilson reportedly advised that the victors should extend the hand of love to the vanquished. Someone accused him of *talking like Jesus Christ.* Would that others had done the same. For the harsh terms of peace placed on Germany made the nation ripe for a demagogue like Hitler. Under his leadership the nation sought to avenge the humiliating restrictions. Who knows how world history might have been changed had those who made the peace *talked and acted like Jesus Christ.*

Lasting Peace

Our nation and the Soviet Union are in a frantic race courting allies among Third World Nations. Our nation spends billions of dollars annually on "hired lovers" (see Hos. 8:9-10). If history teaches us any one lesson, it is that such will not succeed in the long run. Temporary safety, yes. But in God alone is our lasting hope and peace. Will we learn the lesson?

You Can't Organize It

Woodrow Wilson's dream for world peace produced the League of Nations, but this organization did not achieve peace. Following World War II the United Nations was formed. This organization provides a forum for debate, but insofar as preventing war is concerned, it, too, is an exercise in futility. The idea is good, but its higher goals cannot be attained when the organization is controlled and engineered by finite, sinful persons. The world will never know a "just and lasting peace" until people and nations submit willingly to the absolute and benevolent will of Jesus Christ.

PERSISTENCE

Our motto should be "More than yesterday, less than tomorrow."

Until God gives up, neither should we.

Toward a Better Tomorrow

In the drama of life some scenes will be tragic and trying. Those who desire to build a better tomorrow are to look beyond what is to what can be through a people who are dedicated to God's benevolent and gracious will.

Keep Climbing

A mountain climber died trying to reach a lofty peak. When a search party found his body they saw that he fell with his face toward the peak. The party's report was, "He died climbing." So should we!

Beyond the Horizon

When the space craft *Challenger* exploded seconds after its launch, the nation was plunged into mourning unlike anything since the assassination of President John F. Kennedy. Condolences poured in from all over the world. For the first time in our nation's history the president of the United States delayed his State of the Union Address.

Yet on the very day of this tragic event President Ronald Reagan declared that following a thorough investigation into the cause of the explosion our national space program would continue. The people of the nation agreed. Why?

The brave men and women of the *Challenger* were but the latest of that long line of explorers who have led the progressive march of humankind. They can be characterized as those who were ever looking beyond the horizon, not content to sit idly by in the narrow confines of present existence. Thus, men and women have sailed uncharted seas, marched through unknown lands, and scaled lofty mountains. When there were no more earthly horizons, they looked out into space. Soon they walked on the moon and gazed at distant stars.

How the world needs men and women with vision who with persistence will stretch our horizons.

Searching Out Opportunities

A man charged with stealing a turkey appeared in court. He told the judge that his action was an answer to prayer. When the judge asked him to explain, the man said: "Well, judge, it was the night before Thanksgiving, and I didn't have a turkey. I prayed for the Lord to send me one. At midnight I still had no turkey. So then I prayed for the Lord to *send me after* a turkey. He did!"

Poor theology, to be sure. But the story does suggest that we are not to just sit and wait for opportunities to come. Sometimes we have to go out and make them.

Labor with Patient Endurance

"The husbandman that laboreth must be first partaker of the fruits" (2 Tim. 2:6).

A husbandman is a farmer, and farming is hard work. Anyone who thinks otherwise has never been a farmer. As someone said, the farmer works "from can to can't." The word for "laboreth" means to work to the point of exhaustion. Furthermore, the farmer works in faith. With all his labor the farmer is totally dependent on God to provide the rain and sunshine that are necessary for crops to grow. Then the farmer waits from seedtime to harvest to see whether the harvest will be good.

Certainly, then, the farmer is entitled to be the first to partake of the harvest. "Partaker" renders a word that means "sharer." Inherent in this figure of the farmer is the idea that the fruits of one's faithful work are not always evident immediately. Eventually they will be visible. We must labor with patient endurance. For in His own time "God . . . giveth the increase" (1 Cor. 3:7).

PRAYER

I have lived to thank God that all my prayers have not been answered [granted].
> —Jean Ingelow

We, ignorant of ourselves,
Beg often our own harms, which the wise powers
Deny us for our good; so find profit
By losing of our prayers.

> —Shakespeare

There are moments when whatever be the attitude of the body, the soul is on its knees.
> —Victor Hugo

Prayer is not artful monologue
Of voice uplifted from the sod,
It is Love's tender dialogue
Between the soul and God

> —John Richard Moreland

Prayer is the soul's sincere desire,
Uttered or unexpressed—
The motion of a hidden fire,
That trembles in the breast.

Prayer is the burden of a sigh,
The falling of a tear,
The upward glancing of an eye,

When none but God is near.

—James Montgomery

I know not by what methods rare,
But this I know: God answers prayer.
I know not if the blessing sought
Will come in just the guise I thought.
I leave my prayer to Him alone.
Whose will is wiser than my own.

—Eliza M. Hickok

God has only one Son who lived without sin, but He has never had a Son who lived without prayer.

More things are wrought by prayer
Than this world dreams of.

—Alfred Tennyson

Satan trembles when he sees
The least of saints upon his knees.

—William Cowper

One man said of another who was an avid golfer, "He needs to spend as much time on his *knees*, as he does on his *tees*."

They never sought in vain that sought the Lord aright.
            —Robert Burns

He who prays as he ought, will endeavor to live as he prays.
            —John Owen

If you would have God hear you when you pray, you must hear
Him when He speaks.
—Thomas Benton Brooks

An Unanswered Prayer

A woman lived in a small house built at the foot of a tall mountain. The mountain obstructed her view and made the inside of the
house dark. She had read Jesus' promise about faith moving
mountains. Taking it literally, one night she prayed that the Lord
would remove the mountain. The next morning the mountain was
still there. "Humph!" she replied. "Just as I expected!"

Striving Together

In Romans 15:30 Paul urged the believers to "strive together
with me in your prayers to God for me." The phrase *strive together*
is a translation of a Greek word that referred to the teamwork of
athletes in the Greek games. We should agonize in prayer alongside others as God's *team* in the contest against those people and
things that oppose God and His work.

We might illustrate it this way. To football fans the heroes are
the ball carriers. But to the coach and ball carriers the real heroes
are the linemen who open holes in the opponent's line through
which the ball carriers can run. They also protect the quarterback
in pass plays and block for the ball carriers to clear out opposing
tacklers. No matter how talented the quarterback and ball carriers
may be, without these linemen they are *dead* insofar as perfor-
mance is concerned.

In the work of the church, if you cannot carry the ball, at least
you can help others do it through your prayers.

Praying Honestly

Many years ago we were in a simultaneous revival in Oklahoma
City. A foreign missionary on furlough was preaching in a nearby
mission. One morning he told me of an incident that had taken

place the previous evening.

Attending this mission were two profane and unsaved men who were bosom friends. At the outset of the revival the other men of the mission agreed that in their nightly prayer meetings they would pray that those two men would be saved. One of the men was saved on the third night of the revival.

The next evening the saved man was in the pre-service prayer meeting. When his time to pray came, he prayed that the Lord would save his friend. In doing so, he called his friend a very profane name. Though saved, the man's habitual language had not yet been changed.

The missionary told me the profane word. Then he asked what I thought should be done. I said, "Nothing. I think he was the only man in the room who was really praying. The rest of you were thinking of nice words to use. But this man just opened his heart to the Lord. In doing so, he used a word that times without number he had called his friend in love."

Though I did not approve of the word, I had to admit that the man was totally honest in his prayer. If ever we are honest with the Lord, it should be when we pray. At times our pleas may even shock us. But God sees our weakness and the earnest intent of our hearts.

An Answer or a Coincidence?

A few years ago Dr. Keith Parks called on our denomination to pray for rain in the drought-stricken areas of the world. Not long afterwards, the first rain in many months came in many of these areas. Was this a coincidence? Dr. Parks rightly called this an answer to this multitude of intercessory prayers.

Pray Out Loud

As a pastor when I called on someone to lead in the benediction, more often than not the prayer was a mumbling monologue. I confess that I kept one eye open so as to see when the one leading the prayer started to move out. Then I would say a loud "Amen" so the congregation would know that the service had ended.

Turn Your Radio On

In our modern electronic age, the air about us is filled with sound and pictures. To hear and see them requires a radio and/or television set tuned to the proper wavelength.

We may fail to see and hear what God is doing all about us because we are not tuned in to Him.

When You Have a Busy Day—Pray

Before the beginning of each day reformer Martin Luther spent an hour in prayer. If he anticipated an unusually hard day, he prayed for two hours. So often Christians let a busy schedule interfere with their prayer times.

The Wrong Target

A Boston newspaper reporter was sent to a church to cover a certain service. In his article he referred to the pastor's prayer as "the most eloquent ever offered to a Boston audience"! Don't you wonder if it did any good?

The Wings of Prayer

During World War II pilots after a mission limped back to their bases in crippled planes. They came in "on a wing and a prayer."

Believers, however, are familiar with "the wings of prayer" by which we may transcend time and space as we lift other persons up before God. These persons may be near or far away. Through prayer we may be in all parts of the world at one and the same time—without ever leaving our homes.

Prayers Make a Difference

Away in foreign fields they wondered how
Their simple words had power—
At home the Christians, two or three had met
To pray an hour;

Yes, we are always wondering,
wondering how—
Because we do not see
Someone—perhaps unknown and far away—
On bended knee.

—Anonymous

That's Not Prayer

The Pharisee (Luke 18:10-14) prayed "thus with himself," as though he talked to his own image in a mirror. His prayer was totally self-centered, a time to congratulate himself for his virtues. Such a prayer, if we can call it that, was not heard by God.

Staying Connected to the Power Source

An automobile has a battery, which is simply stored-up energy, that enables the machine to function. The motor, lights, radio, and so on draw energy out of the battery.

However an automobile also has a generator that replaces the energy drawn from the battery. If the generator does not function properly, the battery will soon be *dead*. Then when you need power to start the automobile, you will find that you have none. Nothing is wrong with the rest of the mechanical equipment. It simply has no power by which to function.

An automobile has a cable connecting the battery to the car's mechanisms. If that cable is removed, the battery still has some power to spare. However, the power is not transmitted to the working parts of the automobile, so the car itself is powerless.

Christians are like that. We expend spiritual energy in ministry. For us to remain spiritually strong that energy needs to be replenished. If not, in a crisis moment we will discover the power is gone.

One the one hand, Jesus said that prayer is the *generator* that keeps our spiritual power constant. On the other hand, prayer is the *cable* that connects us to the omnipotence of God.

PREACHING/PREACHERS

Just Looking

Dr. George W. Truett jokingly said, "Many preachers are just like Abraham. They spend much of their time 'looking for a field' " (see Gen. 23).

A Poor Shot

Simply because a preacher (or teacher) preaches over the congregation's head does not mean he is using superior ammunition. It may mean he is just a poor shot!

Keep it Simple

Many years ago our church observed what we called at that time "Junior Sunday." I preached on "Jesus Was a Junior," using the event when Jesus was in the Temple at age twelve. I designed the sermon to speak to children 9-12 years old. After the service the chairman of the deacons told me he got more out of that sermon than any other he had heard me preach. To protect my ministerial dignity, I responded in jest, "Well, deacon, I pitched that sermon at a twelve-year-old mind. I guess that just about hit your level." We both laughed. But I also learned a lesson that day about preaching. Keep the message clear and plain.

Whose Choice?

No person should *choose* the ministry as a profession. Rather the person is to be chosen of God to serve in the calling. Since the person has been chosen by God and not another person, the person who has been called is responsible to God alone. The message is to be God's message to humankind. And having declared it, the results are to be left to God.

Get Ready to Preach

A preacher began his sermon with an apology. "Friends, I have been so busy this week that I have not had time to prepare my sermon. I will just have to depend on the Lord today and will try to do better next Sunday." He had the matter backwards. He should have said, "I will depend on the Lord at all times, prepare myself for the task, and He will enable me to succeed."

Joy of Preaching

I have never preached a sermon without feeling how inadequate I was to do so. But once I got into the sermon, with a sense of the Lord's presence, preaching was and is the joy of my life.

Turning the Preacher Off

During the darkest days of World War II defeat by our enemies appeared to be a shocking possibility. Hitler had conquered western continental Europe. Invasion of England seemed near. Allied forces were retreating in North Africa. American forces had been driven out of the Philippines.

At that time I was pastor of Emmanuel Baptist Church in Alexandria, Louisiana, the most concentrated troop-training area in the nation. We learned that many of the troops had battery-powered radios. In an effort to reach these young men with the gospel, the church purchased time for a live broadcast of the Sunday night worship service.

At nearby Louisiana College an elderly lady worked in the college dining room. She regularly tended the table of Miss Hattie Strother, the dean of women at the college. This lady also was a faithful listener to the broadcast. Each Monday morning she would talk enthusiastically to Miss Strother about the previous evening service.

During this dire world situation I saw a cartoon in an out-of-town newspaper of Uncle Sam kneeling in prayer at the front pew in a church. The following Sunday night I preached on "Uncle Sam at the Mourner's Bench." In the sermon I ran the gamut of the sins of the nation. My theme was that unless our nation repented of its sins, God would not permit us to win the war. The message made quite an impression in the area.

The next morning the lady in the college dining room said nothing to Miss Strother about the sermon. So Miss Strother asked her if she had heard it. The lady said, "I heard a part of it." Miss Strother expressed surprise. "I thought you liked to hear Dr. Hobbs preach." "Yes, I do," the lady replied. "Well, why did you not hear all of it?" Miss Strother inquired. The lady answered, "Well, Miss Hattie, I knew he was telling the truth, and I was scared to death! So I just turned him off!"

Improving Modern Preaching

A noted teacher of preaching was asked what one suggestion he would make to improve modern preaching. His reply was simple but striking: "Say 'ye' not 'they.'" In other words, make it personal.

The Object of Preaching

Many pulpit stands have the words "Sir, we would see Jesus" (John 12:21) engraved on them, as a reminder to the preacher that that is what the congregation needs to see in the sermon.

The Goal in View

In 1959 Ramsey Pollard and I, together with our wives, made a mission tour around the world. While in Korea we preached in revival meetings. Missionary Don Jones told us the Korean pastors were surprised at the simplicity of our sermons—the simple plan of salvation. They felt sermons should be philosophical discourses.

Of Ramsey one Seoul pastor said, "Why all he talks about is Jesus." I told Ramsey that was the greatest of compliments about his preaching. After all, is not that the goal of all preaching?

Boss or Leader?

When our son Jerry was a small boy, I expressed to his mother my hope that the church where I was pastor would do a certain thing. He asked, "Well, Daddy, aren't you the *boss*?" I thought, "Oh, son, if you only knew!"

The pastor is not the boss, but he is to be the leader. However, there can be no effective leadership without willing "followship."

At Least He Saw Something

A man had an illiterate pastor. When someone questioned him about it, the man said, "Well, I'd rather hear a preacher say, 'I seen,' who saw something, than to hear one say, 'I saw,' who ain't saw nothin'."

Preachers Need to Be Fed, Too

Billy Graham once told me how he planned to spend a three-month period in which he had scheduled no engagements. "In my library I have a long shelf filled with books of sermons sent to me by various publishers. I plan to read every one of them. I must feed my own soul if I am to minister to others."

Preaching That Meddles

I have known many people who became angry at the preacher because he got on their sins. Someone said that preachers can preach against sin and not get into trouble unless they *name* it. They can really get into trouble when they start applying it. Some people call it meddling. But knowing my sins, I figure if my preacher does not get on some of them he is not doing much preaching. Too many people want a nice little *sermonette* by a nice little *preacherette* to a nice little *congregationette*. What we need is the solid food of the gospel.

Helpful Preaching

Looking back over my preaching ministry, the choicest comment on a sermon came while preaching on the need for sexual restraint from 1 Corinthians 6. A dear lady, eighty-nine years of age with an impish smile and a twinkle in her eyes, said, "Well, this sermon came a little late in life for me, but maybe it will help some of the others."

Offering the Invitation

Dr. R. G. Lee often admonished congregations thus prior to the invitation: "If I were a surgeon performing open-heart surgery on one of your loved ones, you would not want someone to bump my elbow. We now come to a far more delicate time when I will be dealing with souls. Let no one bump my elbow by leaving or creating any other distraction."

A Comforting Explanation

A preacher was the pulpit guest in a church one Sunday. After the service a small boy said to him, "You can't preach a lick!" Naturally this upset the preacher. A layman didn't hear the comment but he saw the shocked look on the preacher's face. So he went up to the preacher and said, "Now, preacher, I don't know what that boy said, but I can see you're upset. Well, don't you pay him no mind. He doesn't think for himself. He just goes around repeating what he hears everybody else saying."

No Laughing Matter

Dr. J. W. Storer, at the time pastor of First Baptist Church, Tulsa, Oklahoma, published a book of sermons. One of the sermons was on the subject of hell. He offered this advice. No preacher should preach on hell, unless he does so with a broken heart. He did not say to avoid the subject, but to preach it out of deep compassion.

Preaching Is Work

A psychologist wrote a book on preaching. He said that in a thirty-minute sermon a preacher expends as much nervous energy as he would in a fifteen mile hike. Certainly such an exercise is to be done with earnestness.

Did You See His Feet

To some people large size can be a handicap. Dr. C. Oscar Johnson was pastor of Third Baptist Church, St. Louis, Missouri, for many years. He was a great pastor, preacher, and Southern Baptist leader. He was of huge stature, not fat, but tall and impressive. Had he chosen to be an actor, his dramatic ability would have made him a great star, but God chose him for the ministry.

When the pulpit committee from Third Baptist went to hear Dr. Johnson, the group expressed ecstasy over his sermon—all except one lady. She said, "He had a great sermon, but I do not believe he is divinely called to preach." Astounded at her remark, a committee member asked, "A man that can preach like that? How can you say he is not divinely called?" The lady explained, "The Bible says, 'How beautiful upon the mountains are the feet of him that bringeth good tidings' (Isa. 52:7). Did you see his feet!"

A Good Question

Willis Howard was my predecessor in Oklahoma City. Typical of his preaching was that at intervals he would say, "Listen. Are you listening?"

What's for Dinner?

A boy remarked that no matter whatever else was on the menu for Sunday dinner in his home they always had "roast preacher." Instead of roasting the preacher, people would do far better to discuss the message the pastor wanted the people to understand.

Relate to the Flock

A church will *endure* mediocre preaching from a pastor who loves the people. At the same time the greatest of sermons will largely fall on deaf ears if the people feel it is not delivered in love. A preacher can preach to people on Sunday only when during the week he has been with them, ministering to their spiritual and personal needs. Otherwise he only will preach *at them*.

I've Heard Some Sermons Like That

One man who spoke little English gave this description of a sermon he had heard: "Big wind. Much lightening. Loud thunder. No rain!"

No Retirement Problems

When I retired I was succeeded by Dr. Gene Garrison. Someone asked me if we were having any problems. I replied: "No. Why do you ask?" He said, "Well, I just wondered since you still live in Oklahoma City and are in the church fellowship." I said: "We have had no problems for four reasons. First, he is a Christian gentleman, and I think I am. Second, I don't want to cause him any problems. Third, even if I want to, I am not there enough to do so. Fourth, my mother did not rear any stupid children. If I wanted to continue running the program I would have stayed on the payroll."

I Can't, but I Know Who Can

Many years ago I turned in my doctoral thesis and left the seminary for a pastorate. At the following commencement I received the degree. Returning home, our cook said, "Well, now you are a doctor!" When I agreed, she asked, "Do you doctor folks?" I said, "No, I am not that kind of doctor." She replied, "Oh, you are one of those doctors who don't do nobody any good!"

Talk about humbling a young theologian! But she was right. I within myself could do no one any good, but I proclaim a Christ who can do every good for everyone.

PRIDE

True pride is akin to self respect. False pride is egotism without a foundation.

Someone has said that "pride in human achievement constantly threatens a prosperous people. Spiritual pride easily leads prosperous people to forget that their blessings are not rewards for being good."

Just as "I" is found in the middle of *sin*, so "I" is found in the middle of *pride*.

> If you stop to find out what your wages will be
> And how they will clothe and feed you,
> Willie, my son, don't go on the Sea,
> For the Sea will never need you.
> If you ask for the reason of every command,
> And argue with people about you,
> Willie, my son, don't you go on the Land,
> For the Land will do better without you.
> If you stop to consider the work you have done
> And to boast what your labor is worth, dear,
> Angels may come for you, Willie, my son,
> But you'll never be wanted on Earth, dear.

> —Rudyard Kipling, "Mary's Son"

Most *self-made* people usually quit before they are finished.

> And the Devil did grin, for his darling sin
> Is pride that apes humanity.
> —Shakespeare

Humanistic Pride

The attitude of humanism relegates God to a place of unimportance in our lives. Its philosophy is, "*I* have done great things today. *I* will do greater things tomorrow." Such an attitude of pride calls for repentance.

He Saw Only What He Did

A small boy on a vacation trip with his family visited the Grand Canyon. The guide told them that the canyon had a depth of one mile. The boy's parents gazed with rapture on this beautiful marvel of nature. As they turned to leave the boy spit out over the rim of the canyon. That night he wrote in his diary, "Today I spit a mile."

Many people focus only on what they do and miss the grandeur that is all about them.

PRIORITIES

Great it is to believe the dream
When we stand in youth by the starry
    stream
But a greater thing is to fight life through
And say at the end, "The dream was true!"

—Edwin Markham

Socrates once asked, "How can you call a man free when his pleasures rule over him?"

If you drive a high-powered car but get on the wrong road, the power carries you farther and farther from your intended destination.

The important thing in life is not so much the rate of speed with which you move but the *direction* in which you are going.

To purchase Heaven has gold the power?
Can gold remove the mortal hour?
In life can love be bought with gold?
Are friendship's pleasures to be sold?
No—all that's worth a wish a thought,
Fair virtue gives unbribed, unbought.
Cease then on trash thy hopes to bind,
Let nobler views engage they mind.

—Samuel Johnson

The Wrong Direction

A motorist driving through the country lost his way. He asked a local resident how far it was to a certain town. The resident replied, "Well, the way you are going it is 24,999 miles. However, if you turn around, it is one mile."

Name Edith's Priority

William Barclay described a woman named Edith who "lived in a little world, bounded on the north, south, east, and west by Edith."

A Study in Contrasts

The crash of the stock market in 1929 wiped out the fortunes of many people. A raft of suicides followed by people who had lived only for material things. These people felt they had nothing left for which to live.

A man who I knew in later years not only lost all he had, but he was $350,000 in debt. Instead of taking his life, he went to his creditors and told them if they would give him time he would repay them with interest. Over twenty years later he made the final payment. At the time of his death, he was once again a wealthy man. He had set his priorities straight.

Defusing a Time Bomb

When I was president of the Southern Baptist Convention, because of the unusual pressures on me, my physician gave me frequent examinations. One day the cardiogram showed congestion in the central blood vessel of my heart. He told me that this was rather common among executives who worked under pressure. Without knowing it, the problem would occur in their fifties and often killed them in their sixties. However, he told me that I had nothing to worry about. He could correct the problem with a simple diet. Two weeks later the congestion was gone. Fortunately, he defused the *time bomb* that was ticking in my heart.

A striking parallel exists between this and our spiritual well-being. We live in a pressure-cooker world in which we are torn between things of the flesh and things of the spirit. Because the world is so much with us, we are in danger of losing our spiritual vitality. We run the risk of forgetting our reason for being.

What's on Your Mind?

A man sat on the second row each night during the revival meeting. He never took his eyes off the preacher, but no matter what the preacher said, the man never changed his expression. He didn't join in laughter at the funny stories; neither did he weep at the sad stories.

This intrigued the preacher, so that he was determined to find out what was on the man's mind. Finally, one night he pointed to the man and asked, "Tell me, what are you thinking about?" Impulsively the man shot back, "Pigs!" Confronted with the preaching of the gospel and all he had on his mind was pigs!

A Fair Trade

Dr. W. A. Criswell remarked to a man about the generous gifts he gave through the church. Whereupon the man showed him a little quotation he carried in his billfold: "He is no fool who gives away what he cannot keep in order to gain what he cannot lose."

True and Lasting Values

I have lived long enough to be convinced that the value of spiritual matters far outweighs the value of material things. From youth through the middle years of life, the temptation is to place emphasis on material values: making money, having what money will buy, and enjoying physical things. Those who become addicted to this life-style may find themselves trapped in it even through life's declining years. Whether or not they admit it, they will find they have settled for an empty and lesser goal. The true and lasting values are spiritual in nature.

REDEMPTION/
ATONEMENT/CROSS

The Father *proposed* redemption for sinners; the Son *provided* it in His atoning death on behalf of them.

Someone said, "The death of Christ did not *terminate*, but it did *germinate* His work."

Those who ignore the cross empty the gospel of all meaning, leaving sinners to wander hopelessly in sin.

On Golgotha, one man died *in* sin; one man died *to* sin; and one Man died *for* sin.

In remaining on the cross Jesus was saying there was nothing in all God's universe He would not do to provide redemption for all who would believe.

Redeemed from the Pit

A few years ago a very small girl in Texas fell down the shaft of an abandoned well. She landed on a small shelf many feet down. Had she fallen a few inches to one side, she would have plunged into the bowels of the earth.

A microphone was lowered down in an attempt to determine her condition. At one point she could be heard reciting nursery rhymes. Skilled and concerned people labored hard and long to rescue her. A tunnel had to be dug down and then angled to her location. The nation cheered as they finally saw a man come out of the tunnel with the little girl in his arms. She had been redeemed from a pit.

It Is Finished!

With a clear voice Jesus uttered one last word from the cross: *tetelestai* (John 19:30). The papyri throw great light on this word. If a promissory note were paid, the one holding the note wrote "telelestai" across it. A deed to property was not in effect until it was dated and signed. When this was done, the clerk wrote "tetelestai" across it.

Another example of its use was when a father sent his son on a mission. The son was not to return until he had performed the last act of the mission. When he did return from a successful mission, he used *tetelestai* to report it.

What do these meanings say to us? In eternity the Son gave the Father a promissory note that He would pay the price for humanity's redemption (see Heb. 10:5-7). On Calvary the note was paid-in-full. *Tetelestai!* The Son reported His completed mission to the Father. *Tetelestai!* Perhaps when the waiting hosts in heaven heard of the completed work of Jesus heaven rang with it. *TETELESTAI!* And the Father smiled His approval.

A Measure of Life

Those who taunted Jesus while He was on the cross measured life in terms of *self-preservation*. Jesus measured life in terms of *self-giving*. His death on the cross was the supreme expression of His measurement of life.

Our Only Security

In 1959 Frances and I visited Hiroshima, Japan, where the first nuclear bomb was detonated over a populated area. In a museum we saw a large stone that had once been part of the entrance to a building. The stone was black except for the shape of a man silhouetted against the stone. This man's body had taken the nuclear rays, leaving the form on the stone. That silhouette reminded me that our only security from God's wrath against evil is to be *in Christ*.

Like a Mighty River

Every mighty river begins with a rill. As it flows along it is joined by other rills, creeks, streams, and rivers, until it becomes a mighty Mississippi or an Amazon. Then even these mighty rivers empty into seemingly boundless oceans.

God's redemptive purpose is like that. Historically it began as a tiny rill—the call of one man. Eventually it will flow like a mighty river into eternity with saved souls that no person can number.

Jesus Paid It All

The idea of ransom should not be construed to mean that in Jesus' death God paid a ransom to the devil who enslaves men. This would mean that the devil is more powerful than God. The thought is that in the death of His Son as man's substitute, God provided the grounds whereby He can forgive sinners without violating His own holiness and righteousness. Since man cannot pay the price for his liberation from sin's penalty and power, God in the person of His Son paid it for man. Jesus paid the ransom for all. It becomes effective for each person who through faith in God's Son receives salvation as a gift of God's grace.

RELATING TO OTHERS

Men's hearts ought not to be set against one another, but set with one another, and all against evil only.
> —Thomas Carlyle

The union of Christians to Christ, their common head, and by means of the influence they derive from him, one to another, may be illustrated by the lodestone. It not only attracts the particles of iron to itself by the magnetic virtue, but by this virtue it unites them one to another.
> —Richard Cecil

> A man who has a thousand friends
>   Has not a friend to spare.
> —Ralph Waldo Emerson

Someone has offered this beautiful description of friendship. "They who have loved together have been drawn close; they who have struggled together are forever linked; but they who have suffered together have known the most sacred bond of all."

> Fame is the scentless flower
> with gaudy crown of gold;
> But friendship is the breathing rose,
> with sweets in every fold.
>
> —Oliver Wendell Holmes

The friend of my adversary I shall always cherish most. I can better trust those who helped to relieve the gloom of my dark hours than those who are so ready to enjoy with me the sunshine of my prosperity.
> —Ulysses S. Grant

O how good it feels!
The hand of an old friend.

—Henry Wadsworth Longfellow

An old Scotch proverb says, "No man can be happy without a friend, nor sure of him till he's unhappy."

God evidently does not intend for us all to be rich or powerful or great, but he does intend us all to be friends.
—Ralph Waldo Emerson

Three Philosophies for Relating to Others

The parable of the Good Samaritan gives three philosophies of life. The robber's philosophy was "What you have is mine, and I will take it." The priest and Levite had the philosophy that "What is mine is mine, and I will keep it." The Samaritan's philosophy was "What is mine is yours, and I will share it." Jesus endorsed the Samaritan's philosophy and said, "Go, and do thou likewise" (Luke 10:37).

Keeping Distance

A West Texas rancher measured his land in sections, not acres. The distance from his front gate to his house was ten miles. When asked why he lived in such isolation, he said, "Well, I didn't want my chickens mixing with my neighbor's chickens."

The Neighborly Find Neighbors

In the pioneer days of the Old West a wagon pulled up at a settler's cabin. The traveler said he was looking for a place to put down roots. He asked the settler what kind of neighbors he had. In turn, the settler asked the traveler what kind he had back East. The traveler said they were cranky, unfriendly, and cantankerous. The settler told the traveler he would find the same kind there. So the man drove on.

The next day another wagon pulled up to the cabin. That traveler also was looking for a place to homestead. He too asked about the neighbors. The settler asked him the same question, "What kind of neighbors did you have back East?" The traveler said his former neighbors were the nicest, friendliest, and most cooperative neighbors in the world. The settler told him he would find the same kind of neighbors there, too. So the traveler decided to stay.

The difference was not in the neighbors, but in the two men themselves. Proverbs 18:24 says, "A man that hath [would have] friends must shew himself friendly."

Common Courtesy

Dr. George W. Truett served as president of the Southern Baptist Convention several years ago. Someone said that in the first session over which he presided, he said, "Now, brethren, parliamentary law is simply common courtesy, and we will operate by it."

Just common courtesy! If we practice it, we will find ourselves rightly related to most people.

A Tale of Two Friends

Damon and Phintias (commonly known as "Pythias") is the story of two devoted friends. Phintias was condemned to death by Dionysius of Syracuse. Phintias begged for a short time in which to set his affairs in order. Damon pledged his life for the return of his friend. Just prior to the time set for the execution, Phintias returned. Dionysius was so impressed that he spared the condemned man's life and begged to be admitted to their friendship.

Who Belongs to Who?

A child became queen of her country. One day from an upper story palace window she watched the throngs milling about their daily business.

Finally, she turned to her lady attendant and asked, "Do all those people belong to me?" The wise lady replied, "No, my child, you belong to them."

Tear Down the Barriers

Robert Frost wrote in his poem "Mending Wall" that "Good fences make good neighbors." That may be true, but fences also may be barriers that prevent us from being good neighbors. These fences are not always made of material substances. Some are composed of wrong attitudes. Whatever the fence is made of, a Christian is to endeavor to remove the barrier through love.

We Do Better When We Understand Each Other

Oftentimes differences arise between people because of a misunderstanding of terms.

Many years ago I was on the planning committee for "The Crusade of the Americas." Our first meeting was in Cali, Columbia. Representatives were there from every Baptist body in North, Central, and South America, plus those in the islands of the Caribbean. Naturally the group encountered some language barriers. The first item on the agenda was what to call this massive evangelistic endeavor. The North Americans suggested "The Crusade of the Americas." The Latin Americans suggested "La Campagna de Las Americas" (The Campaign of the Americas"). Because we had to use interpreters and each Latin American country had to be heard, the debate lasted all day.

Finally, late in the afternoon one Latin American said, "The reason we object to calling it a 'crusade' is that in our country the word *crusade* is a military term. 'Campaign' is a spiritual term."

The North Americans began to laugh. Someone from our group explained that in North America the opposite was true. All day long we had been arguing for the same thing. Only we did not know it. So we quickly agreed that each would use its own terms—different words meaning the same thing.

Turn the Foxes Loose

A man had some prized foxhounds. One day they got into a fight. The man saw his prized dogs literally chewing up one another. Unable to stop the fight, he remembered that he had a fox in a pen. When he loosed the fox, the dogs forgot their differences as together they took out after the fox. Fighting dogs do not hunt, and hunting dogs do not fight.

Transfer the figure to people, and the meaning is the same. We need to turn loose more *foxes* in our churches and denomination.

Problems in Christian Relations

The Christian does not live in isolation. He is related to the outside world and to the Christian fellowship of which he is a part. It is tragic when Christians do not live the spirit of Christ before the world. But it is doubly so when they do not so live in relationship to other Christians.

The average person is more courteous and considerate toward strangers than he is toward his own family. Likewise the average Christian is more thoughtful of others in the larger sphere of life than he is of his fellow-Christians. A man may be cooperative in his civic club but uncooperative in his church.

A Christian should be led of the Holy Spirit wherever he is. If this be true, then his life is a testimony to God's glory in his every relationship of life.

REPENTANCE

There is hope for a person who feels sorrow for sin.

If the past provides a criterion, and it does, unless our nation puts its house in order—economically, morally, and spiritually—we are headed for the graveyard of history.

Be Glad It Hurts

I recall hearing a doctor say, "So long as a diseased appendix hurts there is hope for a safe removal. The danger period is when it stops hurting. It may mean the appendix has burst, spreading poison throughout the entire body." So be glad that when you sin, your conscience still hurts and leads you toward repentance.

"The Hidden Line: The Destiny of Men"

There is a time, we know not when,
A point we know not where,
That marks the destiny of men
To glory or despair.
There is a line by us unseen,
That crosses every path;
The hidden boundary between
God's patience and His wrath.
To pass that limit is to die,
To die as if by stealth;
It does not quench the beaming eye,
Or pale the glow of health.
The conscience may be still at ease,
The spirits light and gay;
That which is pleasing still may please,
And care be thrust away.
But on that forehead God has set
Indelibly a mark,

Unseen by man, for man as yet
Is blind and in the dark.
And yet the doomed man's path below
May bloom as Eden bloomed;
He did not, does not, will not know,
Or feel that he is doomed.
He knows, he feels that all is well,
And every fear is calmed;
He lives, he dies, he wakes in hell,
Not only doomed, but damned.
Oh! where is that mysterious bourne
By which our path is crossed;
Beyond which, God himself hath sworn,
That he who goes is lost.
How far may we go on in sin?
How long will God forbear?
Where does hope end, and where begin
The confines of despair?
An answer from the skies is sent;
"Ye that from God depart,
While it is called today, repent,
And harden not your heart."

—J. Addison Alexander

RESURRECTION

One of the strongest arguments for Jesus' resurrection is that His followers did not expect it.

Guarding the Empty Tomb

As Jesus' enemies placed a guard armed with swords before the sealed tomb to see that His friends did not take His body out, so His friends, armed with faith and fact, must ever stand guard before the empty tomb to see that His enemies never again place His body therein.

Reasons for Not Visiting the Empty Tomb

After Mary Magdalene left the tomb (John 20:17-18) there is no evidence that any believer ever returned to it. Furthermore, there is no Gospel evidence that any of the enemies of Jesus ever visited the tomb. His enemies did not go because they were *afraid* it was empty. Jesus' friends did not return to the tomb because they *knew* it was empty!

Satan Couldn't Keep Him!

A story says that when the crucified body of Jesus was placed in the tomb that Satan sent his demons to guard the tomb to assure that Jesus did not come out. On the third day the demons returned to their master with this report. "We could not hold Him! He got away!"

I Know He Lives!

A Christian woman was asked by an unbeliever, "How do you know Jesus is alive?" She replied, "Because I was talking with Him this morning."

What Is Your Verdict?

Many years ago in my little book *Messages on the Resurrection*, I suggested that 1 Corinthians 15 could be better understood by imagining a courtroom scene. Your faith in the bodily resurrection is on trial. A trial by jury is being held. The jury consists of the minds and hearts of those persons who are unsure about the matter. God is the judge. The accusers are those who deny the resurrection. The prosecuting attorneys are certain Greek philosophers who say that in eternity our souls have no bodies. The attorney for the defense is Paul.

In 1 Corinthians 15:1-11, Paul presented his case. He cited the fulfillment of Scriptures, and he called witnesses to testify to the events. Finally, he addressed the jury as he applied the evidence and testimony to the area of human experience. He closed with strong logic that called for a favorable verdict (vv. 12-58). Then he left the case in the hands of the jury. If you were on the jury, what is your verdict?

SALVATION

If there is no repentance and no faith, there is no salvation.

Jesus is not in the business of saving *good* people but *lost* ones.

Only God Could Do It

The gospel is not a system of reason. It is the message about a person, Jesus Christ, and His redemptive work. Because humankind could not be saved by reason or worldly wisdom God provided salvation in His Son.

Taking God at His Word

Saving faith is simply taking God at His word. Someone asked Charles H. Spurgeon how he knew he was saved. He replied, "Jesus promised that if I would believe in Him He would save me. I have trusted in Him. A gentleman keeps his word. My Savior is a gentleman."

First Get Right with God

Many years ago I read a statement by Dr. Carl Jung of Switzerland. He said that in thirty-five years of counseling people with personal problems, none of them had gotten right with themselves until first they got right with God.

The Source of Salvation Life

Long ago Chrysostom, a fourth-century monk and theologian from Antioch, noted the contrast between the bread and life referred to by Jesus in John 6:32-33. Chrysostom said that manna gave nourishment (*trophe*) but not life (*zoe*). Manna nourished physical life (*bios*), but it did not give spiritual or salvation life (*zoe*). Salvation life comes from the true bread, the One who came down from heaven.

Death-bed Regeneration

A lost person should not presume on being saved in a last-minute, death-bed regeneration. But at the same time, no matter what one's sins may be, a person should not give up hope. Jesus is ever ready to save those who turn to Him in repentance and faith——even as the moment of death looms near.

SATAN

Going His Way

An agnostic said, "I don't believe in the devil. I've never met him." A Christian replied, "You're right. You haven't met the devil. You don't *meet* anybody when you are going the same way."

He Knows the Right Bait

Satan baits his hook with what we find the hardest to resist. He may appeal to either our flesh or our spirit. Normally Satan appeals to the flesh. If we fail to bite the bait, then he changes to some type of spiritual lure such as pride, prejudice, or censorious criticism. We often say Satan tempts us in our lower nature. I would say he tempts us in our higher nature, seeking to get us to express it in a lower way. For example, self-preservation is a basic drive. Satan endeavors to lead us to pervert that drive into hostile and quarrelsome action.

The Devil's Strategy

The devil is too wise a strategist to waste time on a sleeping church. After all, that kind of church is not a problem for him. However he will attempt to destroy a church that is doing a great work for God. Someone said that if you build a cathedral to God the devil will build a chapel alongside it.

That's the Truth

A woman had the reputation of always being able to say something good about everyone, no matter how worthless the person might be. When asked what she could say good about the devil, she replied, "Well, he's always on the job."

SECOND COMING

Encourage One Another

Someone said, "Believers should not worry about when Christ is coming, but should encourage one another because they are certain He is coming."

A Certain Event

One Sunday I preached on the Lord's return, a sermon in which I spoke of the certainty of the event but of uncertainty as to the time. After the service a fine Christian doctor said to me, "Pastor, I agree with everything you said. It occurred to me, however, that even if Jesus delays His final return, I know by the actuarial tables that sometime during the next fifty years He probably will come for me."

I also agree with him with this one refinement. In death I will go to be with the Lord. In His return the Lord comes to receive unto Himself both living and dead believers in their transformed and/or resurrection bodies. So shall we ever be with the Lord.

Ready for His Coming

William Barclay relates this anecdote in his discussion of 1 Thessalonians 5:11. An old Scotsman was nearing the end. Someone offered to comfort him. He replied, "Ah theekit (thatched) ma hoose when the weather was warm."

Have you? Are you helping others to do the same?

Condition over Time

Jesus never spoke of His return in terms of *time* but of *condition*. We are to be busy preparing the *condition* (see Matt. 24:14) and leave the *time* with God (see Acts 1:7).

Predictions of His Coming

In the late summer of 1988 a man predicted that the rapture would occur on a particular day in September of that year. The prediction received extensive news coverage. However, the rapture did not occur.

About the same time I received a letter from a woman in North Carolina. She enclosed charts and figures by which she predicted that the rapture would take place in September of one of three dates in the early 1990's. I guess we will have to wait on her predictions.

We can know this for certain. Jesus will come again.

Doing Just As He Expected

Someone asked John Wesley what he would do if he knew his Lord would return at that time the next day. He said in effect, "I would go to bed and go to sleep; wake up in the morning, and go on with my work, for I would want Him to find me doing what He had appointed."

Recipients of Great Joy

I watched as my favorite college team won the mythical national championship in football. Team members and fans alike rejoiced in the achievement. However, the greatest joy came to those who had suffered the bumps, bruises, and hurts in actually playing the game.

Likewise at the Lord's return the greatest joy will be for those who have striven and suffered for Christ in the interim prior to His return.

SERVICE

No one is ready to lead until he is willing to serve."
—Alfred W. Martin

Too often we use the word *faith* to cover up *sanctified laziness.*

To tolerate misery among men without feeling the call to remedy it, is to fall under the reprobation—"Inasmuch as ye did it not . . . ye did it not to Me" [Matt. 25:45].
—Bishop Charles Gore

> God, who registers the cup
> Of mere cold water for His sake
> To a disciple rendered up,
> Disdains not His own thirst to slake
> At the poorest love was ever offered.

—Robert Browning

God has no perfect individuals or institutions through which to do His work. He has to get along with us just the way we are the best He can.
—W. O. Carver

God can hit straight licks with crooked sticks.
—J. B. Gambrell

The most solid comfort one can fall back upon is the thought that the business in one's life is to help in some small way to reduce the sum of ignorance, degradation, and misery on the face of this beautiful earth.
—George Eliot

God does not comfort us to make us comfortable but to make us

comforters.
—Alexander Nowell

The Fruit of Redemption

If we liken the Christian experience to a plant, we may say that good works are not the *root* but the *fruit* of redemption.

God Works Through Us

To question one's fitness for God's work on the basis of his/her own ability is to ignore the power of God. Whom the Lord calls, He prepares and empowers. We are not to rely on our own sufficiency. In that respect no one would ever answer the Lord's call. The issue is not what I can do *for* God; it is what God can do *through* me.

You Can't, God Can

I recall the time I asked a lady to teach a Sunday School class. She said, "Pastor, I can't teach." I thought I would shock her as to what she had just said. So I replied, "In other words, you are telling me that you do not have enough sense to teach? If I said that about you, you would be terribly hurt. Yet you are saying that very thing about yourself. Actually, you have everything that is humanly necessary to make an excellent teacher. The only thing you lack is the willingness to try. If you will agree to try, God will enable you to succeed." She did, and she made a wonderful teacher.

Those Who Don't Fail, Never Tried

If you are willing to try whatever the Lord tells you to do, He will be with you to enable you to do it. Are you afraid of failure? Are you simply playing it safe by not trying? Thomas A. Edison failed many, many times before he invented the light bulb. Babe Ruth struck out more times than he hit home runs. But they both tried—and succeeded.

Unharnessed Power

The greatest unharnessed power I know is not mighty rivers, but the multitude of Christians who have not been enlisted, trained, and utilized. Failure at this point is one of the greatest hindrances to the progress of the kingdom of God.

Do Your Part

Some church members refuse to assume their proper responsibility in church life. A mother complains because her child has no Sunday School teacher. But she refuses to teach. Others make demands of the pastor and want expanded church ministries. But these same persons often do not give as they are able to pay for the things they want. Someone said that the kicking mule is not helping to pull the load. Complaining, critical church members seldom do their part to make the church thrive. Their complaints and criticisms are but a smoke screen to cover up their own failures.

Use It or Lose It

Kierkegaard told a parable of a wild duck that became exhausted in the annual migration and was left behind by the other ducks. The duck landed in a farmer's barnyard where it was fed daily and associated with the tame ducks.

For a while, every time a flock of wild ducks flew over the barnyard, the duck had the urge to join them. But since life was so easy in the barnyard, it stayed. During all this time, the duck did not fly.

The next year a flock of wild ducks flew over. The "call of the wild" was so strong that the duck was determined to join them. Alas, when it tried to fly it, it could no longer do so. The duck had lost the ability by failing to use it.

The Importance of Vigilance

The famous pianist Ignace Paderewski practiced many hours every day. When he was asked why, he replied, "If I fail to practice one day, I notice it. If I fail to practice two days, the critics notice it. If I fail to practice three days, everyone notices it." Constant vigilance and service for the Lord are necessary if a person is to use his or her talents effectively.

Precious Few

In an interview a businessman was asked, "How many employees work here?" He replied, "Very few!"

If someone asked that question about your church, what would the reply be? In many cases the "precious few" carry the load.

Service Expresses Concern

The house of a neighborhood family burned to the ground and all their possessions were destroyed. A group of neighbors stood about the ruins saying, "I'm so sorry." Finally, one neighbor said, "I'm sorry twenty dollars worth. How about some of the rest of you?"

To be sorry is one thing. To do something about it says how much we really care.

Different Ways to Serve

Not all have the same talents. Each person can serve with the skill he or she possesses and as needs require. For example, there are times when the church needs a plumber who can repair a broken pipe more than it needs a pastor to pray over it.

He Caught the Spirit of Christ

John A. Broadus was one of the founders, professors, and later president of The Southern Baptist Theological Seminary. In those days it was customary for guests to place their shoes outside their bedroom door at night to be picked up and polished by a servant. For several nights a guest in Broadus' home who followed this custom never failed to find his shoes freshly polished each morning. Finally one night, when he heard someone come for the shoes outside the door, the guest decided to thank the servant for his services. When he opened the door a man was stooping over to pick up the shoes. The guest discovered that the *servant* was none other than Doctor Broadus himself! The great man had caught the spirit of Christ and had become as one who serves.

What Are You Doing with What You've Got?

After a service a cultured lady criticized Dwight L. Moody for his poor use of grammar. The evangelist replied, "You seem to use grammar well enough. What are you doing with it for the Lord?"

Agape-type Service

Many years ago we had a stewardship banquet in our church in Oklahoma City. I said to the guest speaker, "In this dining room tonight is perhaps the wealthiest woman in Oklahoma. Can you pick her out of this crowd?" When he failed, I pointed to a little lady moving from table to table pouring coffee. "That is she." She was demonstrating true *agape* service.

Achieving Kingdom Greatness

A child is helpless and unable to reward the one who renders a favor or service. Thus to serve a little child who cannot enhance a person's stature or opportunity for recognition is to serve with no expectation of reward (see Luke 9:47-48). The apostles thought of ruling masses of people; Jesus spoke of serving one little child. In effect Jesus said that if you forget self-glory to serve in His name one whom the world regards with little importance, you will achieve kingdom greatness.

He Knew His Craft

I will never forget the first time I met Mr. Kraft of the Kraft Cheese Company. One Sunday I preached at the North Shore Baptist Church, Chicago, where Mr. Kraft was a member. On this particular Sunday, Frances and I had been picked up at the hotel and taken to the church late in the Sunday School hour. On entering the educational building we were introduced to Mr. Kraft.

And what was he doing? Since the regular Sunday School secretary was absent, Mr. Kraft was using a stubby pencil to figure up the attendance report for that day.

I thought of his worldwide cheese empire with its thousands of clerks and secretaries. Yet there he was, having stepped down from directing a giant corporation to serve as secretary drawing up this simple Sunday School report. His greatness was seen in his willingness to perform lowly service for the Lord.

Ministry Goes On

I retired from the *pastorate* January 1, 1973. I did not retire from the ministry. I will do that only when He who called me into the ministry says, "It is enough. Come up higher."

On the first day of retirement Frances asked, "Do you feel any different?" I said, "Well, for the first time in forty-four years I can put the car in the garage at night without wondering if I will need to take it out before daylight." Yet if the call came I would still go—not as pastor but as a friend.

Choose Your Approach

You can perform Christian service in two ways. One is sort of mechanical,simply carrying out an assigned task. For instance, you are given a card bearing the name of a prospective member for your class or for the church. You make the visit but only as an assigned task.

You make the visit but no one is home. So you write on the card "Not at home" and return it. Mission accomplished! Or was it? Actually, the card screams, "No concern."

The other approach to service is one of concern. This approach is motivated by a genuine compassion for people. This method is the only one worthy of the name "Christian."

The Joy of Being Used by God

When I was pastor of Dauphin Way Baptist Church, Mobile, Alabama, Dr. R. G. Lee preached for us in a revival meeting.

Crowds attended and the visible results were many. We closed the meeting on Monday night when Dr. Lee preached "Pay Day Some Day." The large auditorium was packed, and several hundred people were forced to remain outside. We gave him what he said was the largest honorarium he had ever received in a revival.

Returning to his room that night, Dr. Lee sat in the dark looking out the window. Across the street he saw the steep steps leading into a large house where as a college student he had boarded one summer. He had spent that summer unloading banana boats to earn enough money to continue his college course. The next morning he described his feelings to me in words similar to these.

"I looked at that old boarding house. I remembered each night I was so tired from unloading bananas I could hardly pull myself up those steps. Then I remembered how God had blessed me in letting me serve Him through the years. As I held that large check in my hands, I recalled the revival, the crowds, and the results. My heart was so full. As tears flowed down my face, I fell on my knees and thanked God for his goodness to me."

From an unpromising beginning God had used Dr. Lee and made him one of the world's greatest preachers of the gospel.

He Can Use the Inexperienced

I was ordained to the ministry in June 1929. In sixty years of ministry I have been privileged to help many people. My first experience was with a couple having marital difficulties. Even though I was the rawest of recruits, my effort in ministry succeeded in saving a marriage. It happened through no skill of mine. At that time I had no college or seminary training. I had never heard of counseling. Being married only two years, I had no experience in such problems. But God blessed and used my effort.

At Least Try

One thing about human nature has always interested me. If I were asked what I thought about enlisting a particular person to teach a Sunday School class, and replied that I didn't think the person had the ability, that person would have hurt feelings, if he or she ever found out what I said. Yet that same person will say the same thing as an excuse not to teach. The better response would be, "Maybe I can or cannot do it, but at least I can try." Those who try will discover abilities they never realized they had. Most of all, they will have the Lord's power working through them.

Nothing to Lose, Much to Gain

Before entering college I was an automobile parts salesman. The only other employee was the department manager. One morning without notice he did not come to work, calling to say he had taken another job.

I was asked if I could do the job. I reasoned, if I say no they will get someone else, and I will continue to be only a parts salesman. If I say yes but later find I cannot do it, they will get someone else—and I still will be only a parts salesman. So I had nothing to lose and everything to gain. Therefore, I said I could. I had to work my head off, but I did it.

Why not apply this reasoning when we are asked to do something for the Lord?

SIN

Someone said, "A major aspect of sin involves rejecting God's leadership in favor of leadership patterns provided by the environment."

Speaking of vice, Alexander Pope wrote:

> Yet seen too oft, familiar with her face,
> We first endure, then pity, then embrace.

The beginning of sin is to forsake God. The end result of sin is to be God-forsaken.

A spiritually starved soul may eat weeds in search of sustenance. People will search for something to fill a spiritual vacuum.

> The sin of lust for wealth and power is a demon that
> takes many forms and drives its victims without mercy.
> And in the end, it destroys them.

Sin: We like to practice it, but we do not want to identify it.

Beware of sin. Although God may heal the cut, sin leaves a scar.

Like Satan in John Milton's *Paradise Lost* (Book IV, line 108), some people say:

> So farewell hope, and, with hope, farewell fear,
> Farewell remorse! All good to me is lost;
> Evil, be thou my Good.

Here's the Answer

I once preached a sermon on "The Baptist Hour" with the title, "What Must You Do to Be Lost?" The answer was, "You must do nothing at all! Just stay like you are, for you are lost already!"

Good Answer

Former president Calvin Coolidge was known as a man of a few words. Whether true or not, the story is told about his attending church service one Sunday without his wife. When he returned home, she asked what the pastor preached about. "Sin," Coolidge replied. "What did he say about it?" Mrs. Coolidge inquired. The president answered, "He was against it."

It's Still Sin

"Some people deny the reality of sin. But to do so is to deceive themselves (1 John 1:8) and to make a liar of God (1:10). Others laugh at sin, but the Bible says that 'fools make a mock of sin' (Prov. 14:9). Still others take pride in their sin (Isa. 3:9; Rom. 1:32). The most dangerous attitude toward sin is to tone down its awfulness. Psychology calls sin maladjustment; biology labels it a disease; ethics suggests that it is a moral lapse; philosophy regards it as a stumbling in the upward progress of the human race" (Herschel H. Hobbs, *Fundamentals of Our Faith* [Nashville: Broadman Press, 1960], 64). But the Bible calls it *sin*.

It Does Matter!

In recent years our nation has been shocked by public exposures concerning the private lives of nationally known persons. One excuse for such behavior has been offered by some: a public figure's private life is his or her own business. Such an argument will not hold shucks, to say nothing about water.

An excuse like that one is a commentary on the moral fiber of our society. Underneath these surface revelations is a cesspool of iniquity. A nation built on such a foundation cannot long endure.

The Course of Sin

The mouth of the Amazon River is forty miles wide. The mighty river's source is probably a trickle flowing from the bosom of the earth. In its long course tributaries add to its volume until finally it becomes a mighty river. Such is the course of sin.

A Blessing or Blight

A reporter asked me during the early days of space exploration if I believed, as some did, that space exploration was a sin. I replied, "Space exploration is not within itself a sin. The possibility of sin lies in what we do with the knowledge gained thereby."

So it is with most achievements. They may be blessings or blights depending on what we aim to do with them.

Look How far in the Mire We Are

Blazoned across the front cover of a popular national magazine was the question, "What Ever Became of Ethics?" At least half of the issue contained articles that dealt with ethical and moral problems that have rocked the nation in recent months.

If a religious journal had posed this question, we might have dismissed it by saying the magazine simply was "doing its job." But when a widely read, national publication produces an issue such as this, it indicates just how far down in the mire we have come as a nation.

Three Most Difficult Words

No matter what language a person speaks, the three most difficult words to utter are "I have sinned."

More Than a Nursery Rhyme

From childhood we have been familiar with the nursery rhyme about Humpty-Dumpty. He was some egg.

Humpty-Dumpty sat on a wall,

Humpty-Dumpty had a great fall.
All the king's horses and all the king's men
Couldn't put Humpty together again.

Back of this innocent rhyme is a tremendous and tragic spiritual truth. We are all Humpty-Dumptys. We have fallen off the wall of God's intended purpose for us. All of humanity's expertise cannot restore us to our former selves or give us wholeness.

Abuse of Good Things Is Sin

The earliest Christmas I remember was the one when I found a pocketknife in my stocking. Excitedly, I opened it, grabbed a piece of wood, and began cutting. About the sixth lick, I cut my finger. The cut soon healed, but more than seventy years later the scar still remains. Nothing was wrong with the knife. It was a gift of love. The trouble was I *abused* the gift rather than *used* it.

In love God has given us the powers of our bodies and minds. Used within His will, they bless us. Outside His will, they harm us.

An Unpopular Sermon

Dr. R. G. Lee preached a sermon in which he got on sin hot and heavy. Afterward an irate lady said, "Dr. Lee, I didn't like that sermon!" Dr. Lee replied, "Neither did the devil, sister."

A Question of Conscience

An oft-heard proverb is, "Let you conscience be your guide." But is this a safe guide in conduct? Conscience simply says, "Do right!" However, your moral judgment must tell you what is right. The mores of society are in a constant state of change. This does not mean *right* changes. What one generation forbade, a later one permits. If a thing was wrong a century ago, it is still wrong. The permissive nature of today's social order does not make a former *wrong* a present *right*.

Since the moral judgment has the final say, it is exceedingly important that it be formed on the basis of God's will as revealed in the Bible. Social mores change, but God never changes.

Right or Wrong?

Through many years as a pastor people have come to me with a question. "Is it right (or wrong) for me to do such and such?" The fact that you need to ask should serve as a warning sign. Things that are not inherently wrong can be wrong for you if you *think* that they are wrong. Even if a given act is not wrong, for you to do it with the thought that it is—or may be—wrong constitutes a violation of God's will for you. And this is sin.

Reaping What You Sow

Because of the natural law of seedtime and harvest, the farmer knows when and what to plant to achieve the desired result. He knows that you harvest wheat if you sow wheat, that you do not sow weeds and reap wheat.

God's moral and spiritual laws work in the same way. You cannot sow sin and reap righteousness, or indulgence and reap health, or strife and reap peace. You cannot sow "the works of the flesh" and reap "the fruit of the Spirit."

But there is a further truth in this law. You reap what you sow in *quality*, but you reap more than you sow in *quantity*. From one grain of corn will come hundreds of grains of corn. Applying this in the moral and spiritual realms, it is no wonder that so many lives are ruined, that the world is in such turmoil, and that uncounted millions of souls stumble on their blinded way toward hell! And all because people live contrary to this benevolent but inexorable spiritual law of God.

A Lesson from Whales

Recently in a television newscast I saw a picture of small whales stranded in shallow water on a beach. To remain there meant death. People stood about them splashing water on their exposed bodies to prevent their being burned by the sun.

Gradually they turned them seaward and helped them into

deeper water where they could swim. However, the commentator said that some of them turned and rushed back to the beach. Why they do this is a mystery.

But it is no greater mystery than the conduct of some Christians who have been redeemed from legalism and sin. Before long, they become entangled once again in them.

Whales were made to live in the vastness and freedom of the ocean. Christians are made to live in the freedom that is in Christ and should accept the responsibilities of their new relationship to God.

Perhaps whales act as they sometimes do because of some unknown element in their nature. But Christians should live according to the nature and will of God.

SUFFERING/SORROW
DIFFICULTY

Kites rise against, not with the wind. No one ever worked his way anywhere in a dead calm.
                    —John Neal

> Let come what will, I mean to bear it out,
> And either live with glorious victory
> Or die with fame, renowned in chivalry:
> He is not worthy of the honeycomb
> That shuns the hive because the bees have stings.
>
>   —Shakespeare

Throughout its history the Christian movement has withstood adversity far better than prosperity.

Sorrow, like rain, makes roses and mud.
                    —Austin O'Malley

God whispers to us in our pleasures, speaks in our conscience, but shouts in our pain; it is His megaphone to rouse a deaf world.
                    —C.S. Lewis, *The Problem of Pain*

Someone said that all sunshine makes a desert.

If there were no cloudy days, we would come to curse the sun.

The ups and downs of the highway make the journey interesting.

Suffering does not *make* men and women, but it reveals them for what they really *are*.

248

God's people may seem to endure *hell on earth,* but that is all the hell they will ever know.

Sorrow gathers around great souls as storms do around mountains; but like them, they break the storm and purify the air of the plain beneath them.
                            —Jean Paul Richter

Tribulation will not hurt you unless it hardens you—makes you sour, narrow, and skeptical.
                            —E. H. Chapin

Although a passing cloud of grief may for a moment hide it from view, be assured the sun still shines and the cloud will pass.

Adversity is sometimes hard upon a man; but for one man who can stand prosperity there are a hundred that will stand adversity.
                            —Thomas Carlyle

    Prosperity is not without fears and distastes,
    And adversity is not without comforts and hopes.

        —Francis Bacon

Each of us has known the dark valleys of life. Some of you may be passing through one now. Notice i said *through*, not *into*. Sometimes we have to pass through the dark valleys to reach the green valleys beyond.

        I walked a mile with Pleasure,
        She chatted me all the way,
        But I was none the wiser
        For what she had to say

        I walked a mile with Sorrow,
        And ne'er a word said she,

But O the things I learned from her
When Sorrow walked with me.
                                    —Anonymous

Strength from Hardship

When the hardships of life come to God's people, they may find in Him strength to endure and grow. It is not what happens to a person but how he/she reacts to it that counts. Valuable violins are not made out of soft pine that has known only warm showers and gentle breezes. They are made out of wood that has endured the cold and storms of many winters. Such wood has character in it. Christian character is not formed by lying on flowery beds of ease, but is the product of treading rough highways in life.

A Storm Cloud Ends

I was raised on a small farm in Alabama. One hot summer, as an eleven year old boy, I was hoeing corn in a field adjoining a neighbor's farm. I was overjoyed to see a dark cloud approaching. I knew if it rained I could go to the house!

The rain did come—on the neighbor's field and right up to the fence between his farm and ours. Only a few drops fell on our field, so I had to keep on hoeing.

I learned a lesson that day that has helped me through many storms of life. A storm cloud ends sometime, somewhere.

You Could Just Give Up!

Some people approach difficult situations like the woman who said, "I believe I'll just give the old hen to the preacher. It looks like she's going to die anyway."

No One Said It Would Be Easy

The lowest ebb in England's fortunes during World War II was the period following the evacuation of the shattered British army at Dunkirk. The Nazi hordes were poised awaiting the order to cross the English Channel to invade a seemingly helpless nation.

Largely armed with words alone, Winston Churchill rallied his people by offering them only "blood, sweat, and tears." History confirms that the people responded heroically to his challenge.

Jesus never offered his people a bed of roses. Instead, He warned them to be prepared to endure danger, hardships, suffering, and even death, as they followed Him and rendered the service to which they had been called.

The Christian and Suffering

The problem of sorrow and suffering defines human understanding. The wicked may bring such things on themselves, but what about the Christian, especially one who loves and serves the Lord?

God does not seal His children in a plastic bag and remove them from the stern realities of life. God's laws work equally for all. The Christian lives in a physical body and is subject to germs, disease, and death like any other person.

But there is a difference. Persons of faith who suffer find strength enough to bear untoward experiences and to grow more Christ-like. Christian people die, but they die physically only to live spiritually. Christians suffer bereavement, but they sorrow with hope.

Stewards of Sorrow

In the spring of 1982, Frances had an extended serious illness that finally involved major surgery. Although she faced great odds, she came through it in good shape. Shortly thereafter I received a phone call from a lady. She and her husband were our dear friends. The lady said, "If I can keep from crying, I want to talk to you. Bill and I are walking down the road you and Frances have just walked." She related the situation that her husband faced. I shared with her the things that had sustained Frances and me. At the end of the conversation the lady said, "I feel much better just having talked with you." We had helped by being good stewards of our own troubles.

It Could Be Worse

Former Southern Baptist Convention president and Arkansas Congressman Brooks Hayes noted that some people always were talking about an impending economic depression. He added, "As I grew up there was always a depression at our house. But it wasn't so bad until *hard times* came along."

A Price of Love

Sooner or later the shadow of bereavement hovers over every family—even those who love and serve the Lord. A physician once told me that death is as much a part of physical life as birth. When a baby is born we rejoice; when a loved one dies we sorrow. Sorrow is one price we pay for love.

Don't Be Hasty to Judge

In my college pastorate a small child was killed in the street by an automobile. As I sought to comfort the bereaved mother, a well-meaning neighbor rushed in and exclaimed, "My goodness, Mary, what have you done to deserve this?"

Many people today regard a given sickness and suffering as the result of a given sin. This may be true, but it is not necessarily so.

Hopeless Eyes

I will never forget a scene that greeted Mrs. Hobbs and me one Sunday as we emerged from a worship service in a Baptist church in Africa. Not only the physical condition of the people, but the hopelessness in their eyes haunt me to this day.

TEMPTATION

Someone said the devil tempts all persons, but an idle individual tempts the devil.

> 'Tis one thing to be tempted . . .
> Another thing to fall.
>
> —Shakespeare, *Measure for Measure*, 2.1

> When devils will the blackest sin put on,
> They do suggest at first with heavenly shows.
>
> —Shakespeare, *Othello*, 2.3

THANKFULNESS

How sharper than a serpent's tooth it is
To have a thankless child.

—Shakespeare, *King Lear*, 1.4

Swinish gluttony
Ne'er looks to heav'n amidst his gorgeous feast,
But with besotted base ingratitude crams and
blasphemes his feeder.

—John Milton

You're Not a Hog, Are You?

A farmer visited a large city. In a restaurant before eating, the man bowed his head in a prayer of thanksgiving. Seeing this, a young man sneeringly asked, "Say, old man, back where you come from does everyone pray before he eats?" The farmer quietly replied, "The hogs don't."

Lacking a Grateful Spirit

A man prayed that God would send him one hundred dollars. A Baptist deacon heard about the man's need. At the next meeting of the deacons he related his concern and the man's prayer. He suggested that they honor the man's expression of faith by taking up an offering for him. They received seventy-five dollars and delivered it to the man. Later the man prayed again for God to send him one hundred dollars. Then he added to his prayer, "Lord, if you don't mind, this time please send it through the Methodists.

Last times those Baptist deacons kept twenty-five percent."

Thankful in All Things

We thank God for the good things that happen to us, but fail to express gratitude for the bad things that because of His protecting grace do not happen to us.

Count Your Blessings

An old adage says that counting sheep will help you go to sleep. For the Christian the better exercise would be to count God's blessings upon you. You cannot exhaust that number. But reflecting on His blessings will bring joy to your heart and drive out worry. Then you will know God's peace—and so, to sleep! Why should you toss sleeplessly when the One watching over you never sleeps—or needs to?

He Didn't Do Enough

Two men were talking about a mutual friend. One was very critical. The other said, "I am surprised to hear you say that. It was my impression that he had done many nice things for you." Replied the other, "Yes, but he has not done anything lately."

TRUST/FAITH

Without murmur, uncomplaining.
In His hand,
Leave whatever things thou canst not
Understand.

—K. R. Hagenbach

To have faith in Jesus means to believe *about* Him, *trust* in Him, and *commit* oneself to Him.

True faith does not *see* and then *believe*. It *believes* and then *sees*.

Isn't it strange how long a night can grow
Ere morning and the dew?
Isn't it queer how black a cloud can blow
Before the sun breaks through?
Faith is remembering ere break of day,
Or ere the storm is done,
That out of somewhere speeding on their way
Are the morning and its sun!

—Anonymous

It is one thing to believe *about* God; it is another thing to believe *in* Him.

True faith not only abides in time of trouble but is strengthened by it.

Love is the crowning grace in heaven; faith is the conquering grace upon earth.

—Thomas Watson

The beginning of anxiety is the end of faith; and the beginning of true faith is the end of anxiety.
>—George Muller

An undivided heart, which worships God alone, and trusts him as it should, is raised above anxiety for all earthly wants.
>—James Geikie

> I will not doubt though all my ships at sea
> Come drifting home with broken masts and sails;
> I will believe the hand which never fails
> From seeming evil worketh good for me;
> And though I weep because those sails are tattered,
> Still will I cry, while my best hopes lie shattered—
> "I trust in Thee."

>—Ella Wheeler Wilcox

If we trust God in the shadows, He will give us light.

Someone has reminded us that "it is cynicism and fear that freeze life; it is faith that thaws it out, releases it, sets it free."

A faith whose flag is at half-mast will hardly be found in the thick of the struggle of life's problems. The flag of faith should be raised to the highest pinnacle and become the banner of God's people.

> She [faith] knows Omnipotence has heard her prayers,
> And cries, "It shall be done, sometime, somewhere."

>—Anonymous

Faith is the adhesive that holds life together.

God Turns the World

A popular soap opera supposedly revealed the way the world turned by presenting the trials and tribulations that plagued its characters.

I prefer the words of Mrs. A. D. T. Whitney: "It is almost always when things are all blocked up and impossible that a happening comes. If you are sure you are looking and ready, that is all you need. God is turning the world around all the time."

Wait and Trust

A woman testified in a prayer meeting, "My son was in the war. I prayed for his safe return. God answered my prayer, and I praise Him for it."

In that same service was another mother who also had prayed for her son's safe return. However, he was killed in battle. Did this mother not have as much faith as the other mother? Not necessarily. For the full answer we may have to look beyond the moment. Perhaps this mother may find that God is working for her an experience that will deepen her spiritual life in such a way that she will receive a greater blessing.

Do not question God's goodness, but wait and trust. In time He makes all things plain.

A Song of Faith

Charles Haddon Spurgeon said that any man can sing in the daytime, but that only the man of faith can sing in the night.

In What Are You Trusting

Between World Wars I and II France built the Maginot Line between itself and Germany. The line was thought to be so impregnable that never again could Germany invade France. However, Germany developed a new type of warfare, and in World War II, Hitler's Panzer divisions rapidly bypassed the fortress. They swept almost unopposed across, France, Belgium, and Holland to the English Channel. Hitler had Continental Europe under his heel. The so-called military might of the Maginot Line became a structure made out of cards.

How often have we trusted in "impregnable walls" that have caved in to the intense pressures of life? True security is found in our trust in the unfailing Lord God.

Faith through the Storm

I first rode an airplane in 1945, flying from Mobile, Alabama, to Atlanta, Georgia. Going and coming the sun was shining, and we had a smooth flight. I trusted the plane, or else I would not have flown in it.

My third flight was to Miami, Florida. The flight down was so smooth. I was sold on air travel. But on the return trip, we had to travel through a terrific storm. Flying through the storm cloud was like flying through buttermilk. The plane bucked and reared. At times I could not even see the wings. Once when we hit a down draft, I did not know if we were five thousand or five feet off the ground. I thought the wings had broken off. I was sure we were falling.

When we landed safely in Mobile, Frances met me at the airport. After I told her what had happened, she said, "I knew something was wrong. You are green in the face."

Well, that experience shook my faith in flying. Until one day I said to myself, "That experience should have strengthened my faith in flying. I now have seen what a plane can endure and still land safely."

A parallel exists to having faith in God. When we see how He can bring us safely through life's storms, our faith in Him is strengthened that He can do it over and over again.

He Didn't *Really* Trust Him

A man pedaled a bicycle across Niagara Falls on a wire cable. Arriving on the other side he found another man who marveled at the feat. The cycler asked the man if he believed he could pedal back across the turbulent falls. The man agreed the cycler could. Nevertheless, he refused the invitation to ride across with him. He believed *about* the man but not *in* him.

Living By Faith

Do you say that you do not live by faith? But you do. It is simply a matter of in what or whom your faith rests. A husband eats food cooked by his wife without having it tested to see if it contains poison. Why? Because he has faith in his wife that she will not try to poison him. You accept paper money as legal tender because you have faith in your nation's monetary system. These are but two of many examples of how you live by faith. Yet strangely, so many people become agnostics where God is concerned. This is but another of Satan's wiles by which he causes people to reject the salvation which a loving, faithful God so freely offers.

TRUTH

The greatest friend of truth is time.
—C. C. Colton

Let her [Truth] and Falsehood grapple; whoever knew Truth put to the worse in a free and open encounter?
—John Milton, *Areopagitica*

Truth Will Win the Struggle

Persons often speak of *defending* truth. Well and good, but truth is not so weak that it cannot defend itself. What is needed most is to *declare* the truth in love. If let loose in the arena of ideas, truth will defend itself. Truth is of God; falsehood is of Satan.

Free the Truth

Truth is not to be shut up in a closed Bible safely hidden within the walls of a church. Truth is to be loosed in the arena of life where falsehood seeks to hold sway. All the blatant attacks of atheists and infidels cannot render helpless the truth so much as do its friends who seek to shield it or to shackle it by failing to proclaim it.

Conflict in Human Knowledge

Someone once wrote that the three realms of human knowledge are theology, science, and philosophy. Each has its own method of research and criterion for drawing conclusions. So long as each stays in its own field of inquiry, there is no conflict. However, when one invades the realm of the other, conflict occurs.

UNBELIEF

Without Excuse

In one of the "Big Three" conferences during World War II, Roosevelt and Churchill were trying to get Stalin to agree with some proposed strategy. When Stalin gave his reason or excuse for not agreeing with them, they said, "That is no reason for your refusal!" Stalin replied with a story of two Arabs.

One Arab asked the other to lend him his rope. The latter replied, "I can't. I need it to tie my camel." The first Arab reminded his companion that he didn't own a camel. To which the companion replied, "I know that. But when you don't want to lend your rope, one excuse is as good as any other."

Excuses offered to God are in the same category. They reveal that we simply do not want to do what He tells us to do.

VICTORY

Victory through Grace

Sometime ago I was told that at Southwestern Baptist Theological Seminary a poll was taken among the students to discover the most popular hymns. "Victory in Jesus" was first and "Amazing Grace" was second. This is an interesting combination. Amid our turbulent times Christians long for assurance of victory over evil forces that plague us. We find that assurance in Jesus—His victory and ours through Him. God's amazing grace made those victories possible and available.

Victory from Defeat

Several years ago during the unrest of the Civil Rights Movement, many church buildings of blacks were burned. The Mississippi Baptist Convention had a white staff member assigned to work with black churches. One morning, he sat in his car looking at the smoking ruins of another destroyed black church building.

With tear-filled eyes, he recalled the words from Isaiah 61:3, "Give unto them beauty for ashes" (KJV). He vowed that with God's help he would do just that for these people. Under his leadership the state convention launched an assistance program. As word spread, other denominations asked to help. Money poured in from other parts of the country. Through the program, burned church buildings in the black communities were rebuilt. Literally, people gave them "beauty for ashes"—"garlands" of victory for "ashes" of defeat (RSV).

The Secret of Success

A military tactician said that battles are won before they are fought. That was his way of saying that victory depends on prior preparation. One general called it "Making a good ready." The same principles apply in spiritual warfare. God in Christ has made all necessary prior preparation in effecting His eternal purpose of redemption to give us victory over sin.

WISDOM

An old proverb says, those who know not and know they know not, teach them. Those who know not but know not they know not, shun them.

Cross-fertilization of ideas produces a better crop of ideas, but sterile minds only produce more sterile minds.

Knowledge and Wisdom

When I was a seminary student I recall hearing of a man with a Ph.D. who ran an elevator in a downtown Louisville, Kentucky, office building. Just prior to my oral examination for the same degree the faculty examining committee failed to pass a philosophy student. I was concerned, thinking the the faculty committee was getting tougher. I asked one of the professors why they failed to pass the man. He said the student was able to answer all the questions about the philosophy of others, but he had no philosophy of his own. Both the elevator operator and the student had *knowledge*; neither had *wisdom*.

Knowledge is a mental accumulation of facts. Wisdom is the ability to use knowledge properly in the ordering of one's life.

Storehouses of Knowledge

Dr. George Cross, a former president of the University of Oklahoma, said, "The reason universities are called storehouses of knowledge is that the freshman bring so much of it to the campus and the seniors take so little of it away."

Learning—Constant Responsibility

Someone said that we should count that day lost in which we do not learn some new thing. Benjamin Franklin stressed the importance of learning when he said, "If a man empties his purse in his head, no man can take it away from him." Alexander Pope sounded a sad note when he wrote, "Some people never learn anything because they understand everything too soon."

We speak of going to a college or university as "getting an education." With the perspective of the years, I now know the greatest value of a college education is not so much the *facts* that are imparted; its greatest value for me was that in college and seminary I learned how to study. There I discovered how to learn.

You Have to Dig for It

When A. T. Robertson died he was regarded as one of the world's greatest scholars in the Greek New Testament. He died one week after I began studying Senior Greek under him. Frances later reminded me of something I said as we looked at him in his casket. I said, "Oh, if only he could have transferred to my brain his great knowledge!" That was not possible. He was in the process of sharing his knowledge with me and others when he died. However, what little knowledge of the Greek New Testament I have came to me just as Dr. Robertson's greater knowledge came to him by crying after it and digging for it. It is thus with all of us as we seek after God's wisdom, too.

WORK

Absence of occupation is not rest;
A mind quite vacant is a mind distressed.

—William Cowper

Hard workers *may* still be poor; lazy people *will* be poor.

There is a perennial nobleness and even a sacredness in work.
—Thomas Carlyle

The greatest asset of any nation is the spirit of its people, and the greatest danger that can menace any nation is the breakdown of that spirit—the will to win and the courage to work.
—George B. Cortelyou

Toil is the sire of fame.
—Euripides

It is better to be a common laborer than a common thief.

Hard work may put callouses on your hands, but it will put contentment in your heart.

Referring to "The Village Blacksmith" Longfellow wrote:

His brow is wet with honest sweat,
He earns whate'er he can.

This is the gospel of labor—
Ring it, ye bells of the kirk—
The Lord of Love comes down from above
To dwell with the men who work.

—Henry Van Dyke

"Go to the Ant"

I have never seen a "boss" ant supervising the work and goading ants to work harder. Each ant seems to work as an individual (see Prov. 6:6-11).

Start a Little Earlier

Rarely a week goes by when I do not fly somewhere. Friends kid me about arriving at the airport so early. I have reached the age when I do not hurry, so I start in time to prevent it. I arrive in time to check in, go through security, and drink a cup of coffee while I read the paper. When they call my flight I am at the gate and ready to go.

But always someone rushes in just before the flight attendant closes the door. I say to myself, "If you had gotten up even fifteen minutes earlier, all that rush would have been unnecessary." Some insist on "a little sleep, a little slumber, a little folding of the hands" (Prov. 6:9-10).

Birds Don't Worry—They Work

Jesus did not say that birds do not work, but that they do not worry (Matt. 6:26). Someone said that God will feed every little bird, but He does not put the food in its mouth. Observing birds, you discover that when not winging through the air or on some perch chirping and singing, they are on the ground pecking and scratching. They are not somewhere worrying about the source of their next meal. They are busy from daylight to dark scratching for it. God provides, but they must be busy appropriating what He gives.

Rust Out or Wear Out

In an Indiana church I pastored during seminary days, I said to a farmer, "You should slow down and stop working so hard." He replied, "Now, preacher, I have worked with farm machinery all my life. I know that it will rust out quicker than it will wear out."

In Oklahoma City I knew a man who worked hard right up to the end of his life. As a matter of fact, he spent the last day of his life in his office and attended two Chamber of Commerce meetings addressing community projects. That night he died in his sleep at the age of one hundred and five! Like the Indiana farmer and his machinery, this man knew that the body will rust out sooner than it will wear out.

We Were Made to Work

Some grandchildren asked their grandmother what she planned to do when she got to heaven. She replied, "Well, I have worked hard all my life. So when I get to heaven I plan to sit in a rocking chair for ten thousand years. Then I'll start rocking just a little bit."

Revelation indicates otherwise. John wrote, "His servants shall serve him" (Rev. 22:3). We will work in heaven, only we will not get tired. Otherwise *heaven* would soon become *hell*, for we were made to work!

The Old-Fashioned Way

A television commercial for a financial institution ends with "We make money the old-fashioned way. We earn it." According to the Bible that concept is good religion as well as good industry.

WORRY

The beginning of anxiety is the end of faith; and the beginning of true faith is the end of anxiety.
—George Muller

Don't Borrow Trouble from Tomorrow

A little girl sat on the curb crying. A kind man thought something awful had happened to her. He asked her what was the trouble. She replied, "I was just sitting here thinking that some day I will be a woman. I may marry and have a little girl like me. And she might run into the street and be killed by an automobile." Then bursting into tears again, she said, "If that happened I couldn't stand it!"

Jesus said, "Sufficient unto the day is the evil thereof" (Matt. 6:34). In other words, we should not borrow trouble from the future. We have all we can handle today. We are to trust God in the *known* events of the present and also in the *unknown* events about to come.

WORSHIP

Let us put by some hour of every day
For holy things—whether it be when down
Peers through the windowpane, or when the noon
Flames like a burnished topaz in the vault,
Or when the thrush pours in the ear of eve
Its plaintive melody; some little hour
Wherein to hold rapt converse with the soul
From sordidness and self a sanctuary,
Swept by the winnowing of unseen wings
And touched by the White Light Ineffable.

—Clinton Scollard

If we do not worship God *somewhere* we will soon not worship Him *anywhere*.

Worship liberates the personality by giving a new perspective to life, by integrating life with the multitude of life-forms, by bringing into the life the virtues of humility, loyalty, devotion and rightness of attitude, thus refreshing and reviving the spirit.

—Roswell C. Long

The Need for Personal Worship

Phoebe Brown was a farmer's wife and the mother of a large family. Naturally her days were spent in hard toil. By the end of the day her body was tired, her nerves were frayed, and her spirit was at a low ebb. But each day about sunset she walked down the road to a favorite, quiet spot among the trees. There she sat through the twilight—meditating and praying. She returned to her family duties refreshed. Out of this experience she penned a beautiful poem. One verse is:

I love to steal awhile away
From every encumbering care,
And spend the hour of departing day
In humble, reverent prayer.
If chosen men had never been alone
In deepest silence open-doored to God,
No greatness ever had been dreamed or done.

Real Worship

Can we really call it *worship* if it is not followed by *service*? It is a mockery to praise the Lord inside church walls unless we tell others about Him outside those walls!

Worship As Only a Habit

Satan was standing outside a church building one Sunday morning. Inside, the people were singing, praying, and listening to preaching. A passerby asked Satan if that did not bother him. With a demonic, sneering laugh he replied negatively. Then he added, "They get that way on Sunday, but they will be all right on Monday. It's just a little habit they've acquired."

God save us from such a habit. Our worship is to make a difference in who we are and what we do.

When We Have Worshiped

A worship service should include adoration and praise, thanksgiving and confession, prayer and proclamation, commitment and surrender to God's will. Anything that does not contribute to these has no place in such a service. For unless our spirits experience the presence and power of God's Spirit; unless we are strengthened, challenged, and motivated in God's will; unless we depart better people than when we came—we cannot be said truly to have worshiped.

Worship Is an Attitude

Worship is more than sitting in a pew as a spectator while the musicians and pastor *perform*. Worship is an *attitude* of heart, mind, and spirit. This is why we should spend the precious moments before the "Call to Worship" in meditation, prayer, and soul-searching. The slogan found in many orders of service is true. "If you must whisper, whisper a prayer."

Worship Is an Art

Our generation desperately needs to recover the *art* of worship. I call it an art because it requires regular practice and participation to be experienced at its best.

Do You Have Idols?

In travels about the world I have seen idols ranging from crudely carved pieces of wood worshiped in the open air to elegant images housed in beautiful temples. The material, workmanship, and location is not what matters, but the concept and purpose represented.

You may say you have never made an idol, neither have you worshiped one. Upon reflection is this really the case? Intellect can become an idol as you sit in judgment upon God, His Word, and His purposes in history. Your body may be an idol if you are more concerned about physical appearance and health than you are about your inner spiritual nature. Business or wealth can come before God and so be your idol. Another person may be your idol as you pattern your life after him/her rather than after God and His will.

Achieving your own goals become your god if they are more important than following God's plan for your life. Popularity is your idol if you are more interested in being accepted by other people than by God. The mores of society become your idol if you care more about fitting in than you do about living by God's eternal principles of righteousness.

It is folly to bow before these and other *idols* of this age and ignore the age-abiding will and way of God.

"How Lovely Are Thy Dwelling Places"

Whether you worship in a massive cathedral or in a pine board building out in the country, it is or should be a "lovely" place because it is where you worship the Lord (Ps. 84:1). You can worship him in the home, in the barn, out under a tree, over a kitchen sink, behind a desk, or as you ride the plow. Of course don't forget the worship service in your church!

Topical Index

275

Name Index

Scripture Index